CALEB ROSS

Software Architecture Fundamentals For Beginners

First edition

This book was professionally typeset on Reedsy.
Find out more at reedsy.com

Contents

Introduction: Why Software Architecture Matters

Importance of Software Architecture in Modern Development

In the fast-evolving world of technology, the importance of software architecture cannot be overstated. It is the backbone of every successful application, system, or platform that we use today, serving as a blueprint that guides the structure, interaction, and flow of information within software. As development practices and technologies rapidly advance, the complexity of software systems has increased, necessitating a solid, scalable foundation that ensures both performance and maintainability.

Software architecture is the first major step in any software development lifecycle. It is where high-level decisions are made about how the system will be structured and how the different components will interact. These decisions significantly influence the overall success of the project, impacting everything from its development speed and efficiency to its future scalability and security. In essence, software architecture dictates the structural integrity of the system, much like a physical building's blueprint determines its stability.

One of the primary reasons software architecture matters is because it ensures that a system can handle future growth. As a business expands, its software must be able to scale efficiently without complete redesign. With a robust architectural foundation, teams can easily add features, handle larger loads, and respond to market changes. Without such planning, a system may become unmanageable, with technical debt piling up, leading to increased costs and risks of failure.

Consider modern software systems like Amazon, Netflix, or Google. These are highly complex platforms, serving millions of users across the globe simultaneously. Their success lies not only in their innovative features but also in the strong software architecture that underpins them. These systems are designed to handle a massive scale, rapid feature deployment, and high availability without crashing. Imagine if Netflix's architecture couldn't support millions of concurrent video streams or Amazon couldn't handle millions of transactions per second. The failure to scale would lead to loss of revenue, trust, and reputation.

Moreover, a solid software architecture can enhance collaboration among teams. In large projects, different teams are responsible for different components of the system. A well-defined architecture ensures that these teams can work independently, with clear boundaries between modules, while still ensuring seamless integration. This modularity not only speeds up development but also minimizes the likelihood of conflicts between teams. The team working on user authentication doesn't need to be concerned about the specifics of payment processing, as long as both adhere to the agreed architectural structure.

Security is another critical reason why software architecture is essential in modern development. With cyber threats becoming more sophisticated, the need for secure systems has never been greater. A strong software architecture incorporates security best practices from the very beginning, rather than treating security as an afterthought. This is particularly important in sectors such as finance, healthcare, and government, where the cost of a data breach can be devastating.

For instance, when building an online banking platform, the architecture must account for encryption, secure data storage, access control, and regular security audits. Without these considerations baked into the architecture, the risk of vulnerabilities increases exponentially, leaving the system exposed to potential breaches. It's not just about building software that works today; it's about building software that remains secure and reliable in the face of future challenges.

Ultimately, software architecture ensures the system's maintainability. As systems grow and evolve, maintenance becomes one of the most time-consuming and costly aspects of software development. A well-architected system is easier to update, test, and maintain, reducing the risk of breaking existing functionality when adding new features. This is especially important in today's agile development environments, where continuous integration and deployment require constant updates and improvements.

In conclusion, the importance of software architecture in modern development is multi-faceted. It ensures scalability, enhances team collaboration, improves security, and guarantees maintainability. Whether you're building a small application or a large-scale enterprise system, the right architectural decisions made at the start of the project can significantly influence its long-term success.

Who This Book is For

This book, *Software Architecture Fundamentals for Beginners*, is designed for a broad audience, catering primarily to those who are new to the concept of software architecture but are eager to understand and apply its principles. Whether you are a software developer, a computer science student, or someone transitioning into the tech industry, this book is for you if you want to understand how software architecture can help you design scalable, secure, and maintainable systems.

1. **Aspiring Architects:** If you are a developer looking to transition into a software architecture role, this book will help you build the foundational knowledge needed to take that next step. It will walk you through the essential principles and patterns that every architect must know, providing practical examples and case studies to help you think like an architect.

2. **Junior Developers:** As a junior developer, you may be focused on coding and feature implementation, but it's essential to start thinking about the bigger picture. This book will help you understand how your code fits into the broader architecture of a system and how architectural

decisions impact your daily development work. You'll learn how to write code that is scalable and maintainable within the architectural framework.

3. **Technical Managers and Project Leads:** If you are leading a development team or managing technical projects, this book will give you the insights needed to make informed decisions about software architecture. You may not need to know all the technical details, but having a solid understanding of architectural principles will enable you to guide your team effectively and ensure that your projects are built on a strong foundation.

4. **Non-Technical Professionals Transitioning to Tech:** This book is also suited for individuals without a technical background who are transitioning into the tech industry. Understanding software architecture will give you a strategic advantage, whether you are moving into a project management role, product ownership, or any other tech-related position. While this book won't turn you into a developer overnight, it will give you the language and knowledge needed to communicate effectively with technical teams and stakeholders.

5. **Students and Educators:** Computer science students or those studying software engineering will find this book to be a valuable resource. It distills complex architectural concepts into easily understandable language, making it ideal for learning the fundamentals of software architecture. Educators can also use this book as a teaching tool in introductory software engineering or systems design courses.

6. **Entrepreneurs and Startup Founders:** If you are a startup founder or entrepreneur with a vision for building a product, having an understanding of software architecture is crucial for making informed decisions. It will help you collaborate more effectively with your development team and ensure that your product is designed to scale as your business grows. This book will equip you with the knowledge needed to ask the right questions, set clear goals, and avoid costly mistakes.

7. **Career Changers:** For individuals making a career switch into technology, understanding software architecture will help bridge the gap

between your previous experience and your new tech role. This book will introduce you to key architectural principles and patterns, making the transition smoother by giving you a clear understanding of how modern software systems are designed and developed.

Whether you fall into one of these categories or simply have an interest in learning more about how software systems are built, this book is written with you in mind. Its accessible language, clear explanations, and practical examples will guide you through the fundamentals of software architecture, regardless of your technical background or experience level.

Overview of Key Concepts

Before diving into the details of software architecture, it's essential to understand some of the key concepts that will be explored throughout this book. These are the foundational building blocks of software architecture that every beginner should be familiar with.

1. **Software Architecture:** At its core, software architecture refers to the high-level structure of a software system, defining how different components interact and how information flows through the system. It provides a blueprint that guides the development process, ensuring that the system is scalable, maintainable, and secure.

2. **Architectural Patterns:** These are reusable solutions to common problems encountered in software design. Patterns such as MVC (Model-View-Controller), Layered Architecture, Microservices, and Event-Driven Architecture will be discussed in detail. Understanding these patterns will help you choose the right approach for different types of applications.

3. **Scalability:** Scalability is the ability of a system to handle increasing loads without compromising performance. In today's world, where applications often need to serve millions of users, scalability is one of the most critical aspects of software architecture. You will learn about different scalability strategies, including vertical and horizontal scaling.

4. **Security:** Security should be an integral part of any software system.

In this book, you will learn about security best practices, including encryption, authentication, and authorization, as well as how to design systems that are resilient to attacks.

5. **Microservices:** This architectural pattern has gained immense popularity in recent years, particularly for building cloud-native applications. Microservices architecture allows you to break down a monolithic system into smaller, independent services that can be developed, deployed, and scaled individually.

6. **Cloud Architecture:** As cloud computing becomes the norm, understanding how to design cloud-native applications is essential. You will learn about the benefits of cloud architecture, how to leverage services from AWS, Azure, or Google Cloud, and the trade-offs of moving to the cloud.

7. **DevOps Integration:** Software architecture and DevOps are closely linked, especially in modern development practices. This book will cover how to integrate architectural design with DevOps processes like CI/CD (Continuous Integration/Continuous Deployment), ensuring that the system can be deployed efficiently and updated frequently.

8. **Event-Driven Architecture:** This is another modern pattern where the system reacts to events rather than following a pre-determined flow. It is particularly useful in systems that require real-time processing, such as financial transactions or IoT applications.

9. **Performance Optimization:** As systems grow, performance can become a bottleneck. You will learn techniques for optimizing performance, including caching, database optimization, and load balancing, ensuring that your system runs smoothly even under heavy load.

10. **High Availability and Reliability:** Modern applications often need to be available 24/7, especially those that serve global audiences. This book will teach you how to design systems that are fault-tolerant, ensuring high availability even in the event of hardware or software failures.

By the end of this book, you will have a solid understanding of these key concepts, equipping you with the knowledge needed to design software systems that are scalable, secure, and maintainable.

How to Use This Book Effectively

This book is designed to be accessible to beginners, but it also provides valuable insights for those with some experience in software development. To get the most out of it, here's a guide on how to use it effectively:

1. **Read Chapter by Chapter:** The chapters are structured in a logical flow, starting with basic concepts and gradually building up to more advanced topics. If you are new to software architecture, it's best to read the chapters sequentially. Each chapter builds on the knowledge from the previous one, so skipping around might leave you with gaps in your understanding.

2. **Hands-On Exercises:** At the end of each chapter, you will find hands-on exercises that challenge you to apply what you've learned. These exercises are critical to solidifying your understanding of the concepts. Try to complete them before moving on to the next chapter.

3. **Focus on Real-World Applications:** Throughout the book, you'll encounter examples and case studies that show how architectural concepts are applied in real-world scenarios. Pay close attention to these, as they provide practical insights into how architecture influences system design in real projects.

4. **Take Notes:** As you read, take notes on key concepts, patterns, and best practices. Software architecture is a complex field, and having notes to refer back to will be invaluable as you start applying these concepts in your own projects.

5. **Review and Reflect:** After each chapter, take some time to review the key points and reflect on how they apply to your current or future projects. Understanding how architectural decisions impact system design in the long run will help you make better choices when you start designing your systems.

6. **Use External Resources:** While this book covers the fundamentals, software architecture is a vast field with constantly evolving best practices. To stay updated, refer to the recommended resources provided

in the book. These will help you deepen your knowledge and keep up with the latest trends.

7. **Experiment and Apply:** The best way to learn software architecture is through practice. Use the concepts and patterns you learn to design small systems and gradually work your way up to more complex projects. Don't be afraid to experiment with different patterns and approaches, as this will give you a deeper understanding of how they work in practice.

Chapter 1: Understanding the Role of Software Architecture

Defining Software Architecture
At its essence, software architecture refers to the fundamental structures of a software system and the discipline of creating these structures and systems. It encompasses the high-level design choices that impact how components interact, how data flows through the system, and how the system achieves its goals in terms of scalability, performance, security, and maintainability. In other words, software architecture acts as a blueprint that guides development, aligning technical decisions with business goals.

When defining software architecture, it's important to understand that it is not just about the code or individual features of an application. Rather, it deals with the broader organization of the entire system, involving decisions that affect its long-term evolution and success. These decisions determine the structure of the software, its modularity, the flow of control, and the interaction between different components. Architectural decisions also encompass non-functional aspects like performance, scalability, and security, ensuring that the system is designed to withstand various stresses and fulfill its intended purpose efficiently.

A simple analogy for understanding software architecture is to compare it to the architecture of a building. Just as a building requires a detailed plan to determine its layout, materials, and structure, a software system needs a design that specifies how its components work together. In the same way that poor architectural planning can lead to structural issues in a building, poor software architecture can result in an application that is difficult to maintain, scale, or secure.

Software architecture is typically defined in several layers, including:

- **System architecture:** The highest-level design that dictates the interaction between various systems, services, or applications.
- **Component architecture:** The design of individual components or subsystems within the broader system.
- **Data architecture:** The organization of data within the system, including how data is stored, retrieved, and transferred.
- **Process architecture:** The arrangement and interaction of processes within the system, including process synchronization, threading, and parallelism.

All these architectural concerns work together to create a coherent, maintainable, and scalable system. Software architecture plays a crucial role in managing complexity in large systems, ensuring that each part of the system serves its intended function and can be updated or replaced without causing widespread disruptions.

The Architect's Role in the Development Process

A software architect is not merely someone who designs systems; they are responsible for ensuring that the technical aspects of software align with the business goals, operational requirements, and long-term vision of the organization. The architect bridges the gap between business stakeholders and developers, ensuring that both groups are working toward the same objectives.

The role of a software architect varies depending on the organization and the type of projects being undertaken. In some cases, the architect is a hands-on technical leader who actively contributes to coding and development, while in others, the architect may serve primarily as a strategist, guiding technical decisions and ensuring consistency across the project. Regardless of the specific responsibilities, the architect's role can generally be broken down into several key areas:

1. **Designing the System Architecture:** This is the most visible aspect of the software architect's role. They are responsible for defining the overall structure of the system, including how different components interact, how data flows between modules, and how external services and APIs integrate with the system. The architect must ensure that the design can support future requirements, handle scalability, and adapt to new features or changes in business strategy.

2. **Ensuring Scalability and Performance:** Architects must design systems that are not only functional but also performant under varying conditions. This means designing for both vertical scaling (increasing the power of individual components) and horizontal scaling (adding more components to distribute the load). This involves making critical decisions on database design, caching mechanisms, and load balancing strategies to ensure that the system can handle large amounts of data or high volumes of traffic without crashing or slowing down.

3. **Facilitating Team Communication:** Software architecture is a collaborative effort, especially in large development teams. The architect plays a critical role in ensuring that all team members understand the design principles, how different components fit together, and the overall direction of the project. They act as a point of communication between developers, product managers, and other stakeholders, ensuring that technical and business goals are aligned.

4. **Ensuring Security and Compliance:** In today's development landscape, security is paramount. Architects are responsible for ensuring that the system is designed with security best practices in mind from the start. This includes implementing encryption, designing secure authentication and authorization mechanisms, and ensuring that sensitive data is handled properly. In industries with regulatory requirements (such as healthcare or finance), the architect must also ensure that the system complies with relevant laws and standards.

5. **Managing Trade-offs and Constraints:** One of the biggest challenges architects face is balancing trade-offs between competing priorities. For example, achieving maximum performance may require sacrificing some flexibility, while optimizing for scalability may lead to increased complexity. Architects must weigh these trade-offs and make decisions that are in the best long-term interest of the system and the organization. This also includes working within constraints such as budget, timeline, and available resources.

6. **Leading Technical Innovation:** A good architect stays up to date with the latest technologies, tools, and development methodologies. They evaluate new technologies to determine whether they would be beneficial to the project and ensure that the team is using the best tools for the job. Architects often lead the adoption of new frameworks, cloud platforms, or microservices architectures, providing the technical leadership needed to ensure successful implementation.

7. **Documentation and Standards:** A critical yet often overlooked aspect of the architect's role is documentation. Clear and comprehensive documentation ensures that future developers can understand the architecture and continue to maintain or improve the system. Architects are responsible for creating architectural documentation that outlines the system's design principles, decision-making processes, and trade-offs. They also establish coding standards and best practices to ensure consistency across the development team.

In short, software architects wear many hats. They are part strategist, part engineer, and part leader, guiding the technical direction of a project while ensuring that it aligns with business goals and operational requirements. Their decisions have long-lasting implications for the success of the project and the maintainability of the system.

Core Principles of Good Architecture

Building software that stands the test of time requires a strong foundation rooted in solid architectural principles. Whether you're designing a simple web application or a complex distributed system, certain principles form the bedrock of good software architecture. Let's explore these core principles in detail:

1. **Modularity and Separation of Concerns** Modularity is the principle of breaking down a software system into smaller, self-contained components that can be developed, tested, and maintained independently. Each module should have a clear, single responsibility (a concept often referred to as the Single Responsibility Principle). This separation of concerns makes the system easier to understand, test, and modify, as changes to one module do not impact others.

2. Modularity also improves scalability. As your system grows, you can scale individual modules independently without needing to redesign the entire system. This approach is critical in large, complex systems, where monolithic designs often become difficult to maintain over time.

3. **Scalability** Scalability is the ability of a system to grow and handle increased loads without sacrificing performance or stability. There are two primary types of scalability: vertical and horizontal. Vertical scalability involves increasing the capacity of individual components, while horizontal scalability involves adding more components to distribute the load.

4. Designing for scalability requires architects to consider not only the current needs of the system but also its potential future growth. This means choosing databases, messaging systems, and architectural patterns (such as microservices or event-driven architectures) that can scale effectively as the system grows.

5. **Maintainability** A good architecture is maintainable, meaning that it can be easily updated and extended over time without introducing bugs or breaking existing functionality. This is achieved through modular design, clean code, and proper documentation.

6. Maintainability is especially important in today's fast-paced development environments, where systems are constantly evolving. Without a maintainable architecture, small changes can result in unexpected side effects, increasing the risk of bugs and slowing down the development

process.

7. **Reusability** Reusability is the principle of designing software components that can be used across different parts of the system or even in entirely different projects. Reusable components reduce duplication of effort, save development time, and improve consistency across the system.

8. To design reusable components, architects must focus on creating generic, decoupled modules that do not rely on specific implementations or dependencies. This allows the components to be easily adapted for different use cases.

9. **Security** Security should be a core consideration in any software architecture. Architects must design systems that protect sensitive data, ensure user privacy, and defend against common attack vectors such as SQL injection, cross-site scripting (XSS), and denial of service (DoS) attacks.

10. A secure architecture includes encryption, proper authentication and authorization mechanisms, and data validation. Security is not something that can be added after the fact; it must be considered from the start to ensure that the system is resilient to attacks.

11. **Performance** Performance refers to how efficiently a system executes its tasks, particularly under load. Good architecture ensures that the system can handle high volumes of traffic, process large datasets, and execute complex operations without significant delays.

12. Performance optimization often involves making trade-offs between speed, resource usage, and maintainability. Architects must carefully consider these trade-offs and implement caching strategies, load balancing, and other optimization techniques to ensure that the system performs well under stress.

13. **Flexibility** A flexible architecture is one that can adapt to changing requirements and evolving business needs. Flexibility is essential in today's fast-moving business environments, where software systems need to be updated frequently to stay competitive.

14. Architects can achieve flexibility by designing systems with loose

coupling between components. This allows individual modules to be updated or replaced without affecting other parts of the system. A flexible architecture also supports a wide range of deployment environments, from on-premises servers to cloud platforms.

15. **Consistency** Consistency ensures that the system behaves in predictable ways across different environments, users, and use cases. This includes consistency in data processing, user interfaces, and system responses.

16. Achieving consistency often involves adhering to established design patterns, standards, and best practices. It also requires architects to define clear rules for how different parts of the system interact and how data flows through the system.

17. **Testability** A well-designed system is easy to test. Testability ensures that individual components can be isolated and tested independently, making it easier to identify bugs and ensure that new features do not introduce regressions.

18. Testability is often achieved through modular design, clean interfaces, and automated testing frameworks. Architects must ensure that the system supports unit testing, integration testing, and end-to-end testing, as well as continuous integration and continuous delivery (CI/CD) pipelines.

19. **Cost-Effectiveness** While performance, scalability, and security are all critical, cost-effectiveness is also a key concern. A good architecture must balance technical excellence with budget constraints. This involves choosing technologies, cloud services, and infrastructure that provide the best value for money without compromising the system's long-term viability.

20. Cost-effectiveness also involves making strategic trade-offs between performance and cost. For example, achieving ultra-low latency might require expensive infrastructure, but a well-architected system can often achieve acceptable performance levels at a fraction of the cost by using caching and load balancing techniques.

These principles form the foundation of good software architecture. By adhering to them, architects can design systems that are scalable, secure, maintainable, and cost-effective, ensuring long-term success.

Balancing Technical and Business Needs

A key challenge in software architecture is balancing the technical requirements of a system with the business goals and constraints of the organization. This balance is often difficult to achieve, as the two sets of requirements can sometimes be in conflict. For example, a system that prioritizes performance may require more expensive infrastructure, while a system that prioritizes cost-effectiveness may sacrifice some performance.

One of the architect's most important roles is to navigate these trade-offs and ensure that the system meets both technical and business needs. This requires close collaboration with business stakeholders, product managers, and other non-technical team members to understand the organization's goals and priorities.

Here are some strategies for balancing technical and business needs:

1. **Align Architecture with Business Goals** The architecture of a system should be designed to support the business's goals and strategy. For example, if the business is focused on rapid growth and scalability, the architecture should be designed to support high levels of traffic and quick feature deployment. If the business is focused on cost-efficiency, the architecture should prioritize cost-effective solutions, such as cloud services with usage-based pricing.

2. To align architecture with business goals, architects must communicate regularly with business stakeholders to understand their priorities and ensure that the system is designed to meet them.

3. **Prioritize Features Based on Business Value** Not all features or technical improvements provide the same level of business value. Architects must work with product managers to prioritize features and technical decisions based on their impact on the business. For example, improving performance in an area that directly affects customer satisfaction may be more valuable than optimizing a backend process that has little impact on the end-user experience.

4. By prioritizing features based on business value, architects can ensure that the development team is working on the most important tasks first, while still maintaining a focus on technical excellence.

5. **Consider Long-Term vs Short-Term Trade-offs** Many architectural decisions involve trade-offs between short-term and long-term goals. For example, using a quick but inefficient solution may help meet a tight deadline, but it could create technical debt that needs to be addressed later. On the other hand, investing in a more robust solution now may delay the release but provide long-term benefits in terms of scalability and maintainability.

6. Architects must carefully consider these trade-offs and make decisions that balance the immediate needs of the project with the long-term health of the system. In some cases, it may be appropriate to take on short-term technical debt, but architects must ensure that there is a plan in place to address it in the future.

7. **Communicate Trade-offs and Risks to Stakeholders** One of the architect's key responsibilities is to communicate the trade-offs and risks associated with different architectural decisions to business stakeholders. This includes explaining the potential impact of technical debt, scalability challenges, security risks, and other technical considerations in a way that non-technical stakeholders can understand.

8. By providing clear, concise explanations of the trade-offs involved in different decisions, architects can help stakeholders make informed choices that align with both technical and business goals.

9. **Use Metrics to Drive Decision-Making** Architects should use metrics to quantify the impact of different architectural decisions on the system and the business. For example, performance metrics, such as response times and throughput, can help guide decisions about scalability and optimization. Cost metrics, such as infrastructure expenses and cloud usage, can help ensure that the system remains cost-effective.

10. By using metrics to drive decision-making, architects can make more objective decisions and ensure that the system is optimized for both technical and business success.

In conclusion, balancing technical and business needs is a critical aspect of software architecture. By aligning the architecture with business goals, prioritizing features based on business value, considering long-term trade-offs, communicating risks to stakeholders, and using metrics to guide decisions, architects can design systems that are both technically excellent and aligned with the organization's strategic objectives.

Chapter 2: Key Architectural Patterns and Their Applications

I **ntroduction to Common Patterns**

Software architecture patterns are general reusable solutions to commonly occurring problems in software design. These patterns are templates designed to help system architects address fundamental design challenges. By adhering to tried-and-tested patterns, architects can ensure that their systems are scalable, maintainable, and flexible, while also solving specific technical problems in efficient and predictable ways.

In this chapter, we will explore several key architectural patterns—Layered Architecture, MVC (Model-View-Controller), Microservices, and Event-Driven Architecture—and discuss their advantages, when to use them, real-world examples, and a detailed case study to illustrate how choosing the right pattern is essential for a small application.

Layered Architecture

Overview

Layered architecture, also known as the n-tier architecture, is one of the most common and widely used architectural patterns. It divides the system into layers, each with its own responsibility, allowing for better organization of code, easier testing, and enhanced separation of concerns.

Traditionally, the layers in this architecture include:

- **Presentation Layer:** Handles the user interface (UI) and interactions.
- **Business Logic Layer:** Contains the core functionality and business rules.
- **Data Access Layer:** Manages communication with the data sources, such as databases.
- **Database Layer:** The actual database or data storage mechanism.

The layered architecture is a highly structured approach that emphasizes modularity, separation of concerns, and reusability. Each layer interacts only with the layer directly below it, creating a well-defined flow of information and reducing dependencies.

When to Use Layered Architecture

Layered architecture is particularly useful in systems where the complexity can be broken down into discrete sections, such as business applications or web systems. This pattern is ideal when:

- The application needs to be scalable, but not necessarily at the microservices level.
- You want to maintain clear separation of concerns, with each layer handling a specific responsibility.
- Teams are working on different layers of the application, so modularity is essential to ensure collaboration without causing conflicts.

Real-World Example

An example of a layered architecture is a simple e-commerce website:

- **Presentation Layer:** The website UI, where users browse products and place orders.
- **Business Logic Layer:** Handles the process of adding items to a shopping cart, calculating totals, and processing orders.
- **Data Access Layer:** Retrieves product details and user information from a database.
- **Database Layer:** Stores all product information, user accounts, and

orders in a relational database like MySQL.

In this system, each layer has a clear responsibility, which makes the system more maintainable and scalable.

Advantages of Layered Architecture

- **Modularity:** Changes can be made in one layer without affecting the others, making the system easier to maintain.
- **Separation of Concerns:** Each layer has a distinct responsibility, which reduces complexity and makes testing simpler.
- **Reusability:** Code within each layer can be reused in different parts of the system or even in other projects.

Disadvantages of Layered Architecture

- **Performance Overhead:** Since each layer has to communicate with the adjacent layers, performance can be slower compared to other architectural patterns like microservices.
- **Rigid Structure:** The strict separation between layers can sometimes lead to inefficiency when the application requires rapid data processing across layers.

MVC (Model-View-Controller)
Overview

The Model-View-Controller (MVC) pattern is another commonly used architecture, particularly in web development. It divides an application into three interconnected components:

- **Model:** Represents the data and the business rules of the application. It directly manages the data, logic, and rules of the application.
- **View:** The user interface that presents the data to the user. It is responsible for rendering the UI based on the data in the model.
- **Controller:** Acts as an intermediary between the Model and the View.

It receives input from the user, processes it (by calling the model), and updates the view accordingly.

The primary purpose of MVC is to separate concerns, making the development process more manageable by assigning different roles to different components.

When to Use MVC

MVC is widely used in web applications and frameworks like Ruby on Rails, ASP.NET, and Django. It is most effective in systems where:

- User interaction is central, and there's a need for a dynamic interface.
- The application requires frequent updates and changes to the user interface without affecting the underlying business logic.
- You want to maintain a clean separation between the data model and the user interface, reducing the coupling between them.

Real-World Example

A common example of the MVC pattern is an online ticket booking system:

- **Model:** Manages the data related to available tickets, user bookings, and payment information.
- **View:** Displays available tickets, booking forms, and confirmation messages to the user.
- **Controller:** Handles user actions, such as selecting seats, making payments, and confirming bookings, by updating the model and refreshing the view.

The MVC pattern allows the system to update either the business logic (e.g., how bookings are processed) or the user interface (e.g., the way tickets are displayed) without affecting the other, making the system flexible and maintainable.

Advantages of MVC

- **Separation of Concerns:** The MVC pattern creates a clear separation between the UI, the data model, and the control logic, making the system easier to maintain.
- **Modularity:** Changes to one component do not impact the others, making development and testing faster.
- **Scalability:** MVC is suitable for applications that require rapid scaling, as it provides a structured way to build modular systems.

Disadvantages of MVC

- **Complexity:** For smaller projects, the MVC structure can add unnecessary complexity.
- **Overhead:** The separation of concerns can introduce overhead in terms of development and management, particularly if the components are tightly coupled in practice.

Microservices Architecture
Overview

Microservices architecture is a modern architectural pattern that breaks down a monolithic application into a set of loosely coupled, independently deployable services. Each service focuses on a specific business function, and services communicate with each other through APIs, often using lightweight protocols like HTTP/REST or messaging queues.

Microservices architecture is widely used in large-scale systems where modularity, flexibility, and scalability are critical. It allows development teams to build, deploy, and scale individual services independently, making it easier to update the system without affecting the entire application.

When to Use Microservices

Microservices architecture is suitable for large, complex systems where:

- You need to scale individual components of the system independently (e.g., scaling the payment service without affecting the product catalog service).

- The application requires frequent updates or additions of new features, and you want to avoid a monolithic system that is hard to change.
- Development teams are distributed, with different teams working on different services, allowing for faster development and deployment.

Real-World Example

One of the most well-known examples of microservices architecture is Netflix:

- **User Service:** Manages user accounts, profiles, and subscriptions.
- **Content Delivery Service:** Streams video content to users.
- **Recommendation Engine:** Provides personalized content suggestions based on viewing history and preferences.
- **Payment Service:** Handles subscription payments and billing.

Each of these services operates independently, allowing Netflix to scale specific parts of its system (e.g., the streaming service during peak hours) without affecting other services. This flexibility is one of the key advantages of microservices architecture.

Advantages of Microservices

- **Scalability:** Each service can be scaled independently, allowing for more efficient use of resources.
- **Modularity:** Services are loosely coupled, so changes to one service do not impact others.
- **Continuous Delivery:** Microservices architecture supports rapid development and deployment, making it easier to roll out new features or updates.

Disadvantages of Microservices

- **Complexity:** Managing multiple services, each with its own dependencies and data storage, can introduce significant complexity.

- **Inter-service Communication:** As services interact with each other over the network, managing inter-service communication (including error handling, retries, and data consistency) can be challenging.
- **Operational Overhead:** Deploying, monitoring, and maintaining multiple services requires sophisticated DevOps practices and tooling.

Event-Driven Architecture
Overview
Event-driven architecture is a pattern in which the system responds to and processes events in real-time. Events are generated by user actions, system triggers, or other sources, and components in the system react to these events asynchronously. This architecture is particularly useful in systems where real-time processing and responsiveness are critical.

Event-driven architecture is composed of two main components:

- **Event Producers:** These generate events when something happens (e.g., a user clicks a button, or a system update is triggered).
- **Event Consumers:** These listen for and process events, taking action based on the event data.

The system uses an event broker (like Apache Kafka or RabbitMQ) to handle the distribution of events between producers and consumers.

When to Use Event-Driven Architecture
This pattern is ideal for systems where real-time responsiveness is crucial, such as:

- Systems that need to react to user interactions in real-time (e.g., stock trading platforms).
- IoT (Internet of Things) applications that need to process sensor data as it is generated.
- Systems that require decoupled communication between components, allowing them to operate independently.

Real-World Example

A classic example of an event-driven architecture is an e-commerce website that handles order processing:

- **Event Producer:** When a customer places an order, an event is generated that triggers the order processing system.
- **Event Consumers:** Multiple services may consume this event, such as the inventory service (to update stock levels), the payment service (to process the transaction), and the notification service (to send confirmation emails).

This architecture allows the system to process orders asynchronously, improving performance and scalability.

Advantages of Event-Driven Architecture

- **Real-Time Processing:** Events are processed as they occur, enabling real-time responsiveness.
- **Scalability:** Components are loosely coupled, allowing them to be scaled independently.
- **Flexibility:** New event consumers can be added without affecting existing components, making the system highly adaptable.

Disadvantages of Event-Driven Architecture

- **Complexity:** Managing event flows and ensuring data consistency can be complex, particularly in systems with many event producers and consumers.
- **Latency:** Depending on the implementation, there may be some latency in event processing, especially if the event broker experiences delays.

When to Use Specific Patterns

Understanding when to use each architectural pattern is key to designing systems that meet your requirements. Here are some guidelines for choosing the right pattern based on your needs:

- **Layered Architecture:** Use when your system can be easily separated into distinct layers, such as business applications, enterprise systems, and web applications.
- **MVC:** Best for systems with complex user interfaces and frequent interactions between users and data, such as web and desktop applications.
- **Microservices:** Ideal for large, complex systems that need to be scalable, flexible, and independently deployable, such as cloud-based platforms or SaaS products.
- **Event-Driven Architecture:** Suitable for real-time systems or those that require asynchronous processing, such as IoT applications or financial trading platforms.

Case Study: Choosing the Right Architecture for a Small Application

Imagine you're tasked with building a small, but scalable, online task management tool. Users can create, assign, and manage tasks in real-time, with features like notifications, task lists, and collaboration tools. Let's examine the process of choosing the right architecture for this project.

Understanding Requirements

- **Real-Time Interaction:** Users need to see updates in real-time (e.g., when a task is completed, reassigned, or commented on).
- **Scalability:** Although the system will start small, it should be able to scale as more users and teams adopt the tool.
- **Maintainability:** The system should be easy to maintain and extend, as new features like calendar integration and reporting may be added later.

Evaluating the Options

- **Layered Architecture:** Provides a structured, maintainable design but might struggle with real-time updates.
- **MVC:** Good separation between data (tasks) and presentation (UI),

but may not fully support real-time collaboration without significant complexity.

- **Microservices:** Overkill for a small application, though it could work well if the tool becomes larger and more complex over time.
- **Event-Driven Architecture:** Ideal for real-time notifications and task updates, allowing users to see changes as they happen without refreshing the page.

Choosing the Architecture

For this small application, an **event-driven architecture** combined with aspects of **MVC** would be the best approach. The MVC pattern would handle the task management functionality, while the event-driven architecture would ensure real-time updates, with an event broker managing notifications and task updates across users.

By understanding these key architectural patterns and their applications, you can make informed decisions about how to design your systems, whether you're building small applications or large-scale platforms. In the next chapter, we will dive deeper into the principles of scalability and how architectural decisions can impact a system's ability to grow over time.

Chapter 3: Architectural Principles and Best Practices

I n the world of software architecture, building systems that are scalable, maintainable, and robust requires adherence to core principles that help manage complexity. By following established best practices, architects can design systems that not only meet the current needs of an organization but also adapt to future requirements. In this chapter, we'll explore key architectural principles and best practices, including SOLID principles, designing for change and scalability, separation of concerns, loose coupling, and the importance of maintainability and testability.

SOLID Principles in Architecture

The SOLID principles, first introduced by Robert C. Martin, are a set of five design principles aimed at creating more understandable, flexible, and maintainable software systems. These principles are fundamental to object-oriented design and are widely applicable to software architecture in general. Each principle helps architects design components that are modular, reusable, and easier to manage, which is crucial when building complex systems.

Let's explore each of the SOLID principles in the context of software architecture:

1. Single Responsibility Principle (SRP)

The Single Responsibility Principle states that a class or module should have only one reason to change, meaning that it should have only one responsibility or function. In the context of architecture, this principle extends to components or layers of a system. Each component should have a clear, single responsibility.

For example, in a typical web application, you might have a business logic layer, a data access layer, and a presentation layer. Each layer has a distinct responsibility: the business logic layer handles the core functionality of the system, the data access layer manages database interactions, and the presentation layer handles the user interface. By adhering to SRP, changes to one layer (e.g., modifying the UI) do not affect other layers (e.g., the data access layer), making the system easier to maintain.

Architectural Impact of SRP:

- **Modularity:** Systems built with SRP are more modular, making it easier to update, maintain, and scale different parts of the system.
- **Separation of Concerns:** By ensuring that each part of the system has a single responsibility, architects can reduce complexity and make each component easier to test and reason about.
- **Maintainability:** When components are responsible for only one thing, changes in the system are localized, reducing the risk of introducing bugs.

2. Open/Closed Principle (OCP)

The Open/Closed Principle states that software entities (such as classes, modules, or components) should be open for extension but closed for modification. This means that the behavior of a component should be extendable without modifying its source code.

In architecture, this principle is vital when designing systems that need to evolve over time. For example, an e-commerce application might initially support only credit card payments, but later needs to extend functionality to support PayPal or cryptocurrency payments. Instead of modifying the existing payment processing code, architects should design the system in a way that allows new payment methods to be added without changing the core system.

Architectural Impact of OCP:

- **Extensibility:** Systems built with OCP in mind are easier to extend as new features or requirements emerge.
- **Reducing Technical Debt:** By avoiding changes to existing code, architects minimize the risk of introducing bugs or breaking existing functionality.
- **Plugin Architecture:** OCP is often implemented via plugin architectures, where new functionality can be added by simply plugging in new modules, making the system highly adaptable.

3. Liskov Substitution Principle (LSP)

The Liskov Substitution Principle states that objects of a superclass should be replaceable with objects of a subclass without affecting the correctness of the program. In other words, a derived class must be able to stand in for its parent class without altering the expected behavior.

In the context of architecture, LSP ensures that components designed with inheritance can be extended or substituted without breaking the overall system. For example, in a web application, if you have a general logging component, it should be possible to substitute it with a more specialized logging mechanism (such as logging to a file or a database) without changing how other parts of the system interact with the logger.

Architectural Impact of LSP:

- **Interchangeability:** Components adhering to LSP are easily interchangeable, making the system more flexible and easier to extend.
- **Reduced Risk of Breakage:** By following LSP, architects ensure that new implementations of components won't break existing functionality, making the system more robust.

4. Interface Segregation Principle (ISP)

The Interface Segregation Principle states that clients should not be forced to depend on interfaces they do not use. In other words, large, monolithic interfaces should be broken down into smaller, more specific ones so that clients only need to implement the methods they actually require.

For instance, consider an application with a single PaymentProcessor interface that includes methods for both credit card and bank transfer payments. If a component only handles bank transfers, it should not be forced to implement methods related to credit card payments. Instead, architects should design more granular interfaces, such as CreditCardProcessor and BankTransferProcessor.

Architectural Impact of ISP:

- **Decoupling:** By designing smaller, more specific interfaces, architects reduce the coupling between components, making the system more flexible and easier to maintain.
- **Improved Flexibility:** Clients are only required to implement the functionality they need, reducing unnecessary dependencies and making the system easier to evolve.

5. Dependency Inversion Principle (DIP)

The Dependency Inversion Principle states that high-level modules should not depend on low-level modules. Both should depend on abstractions, and abstractions should not depend on details. This principle emphasizes that code should rely on interfaces or abstract classes, not concrete implementations.

In architecture, DIP is crucial for creating loosely coupled systems. For example, instead of hard-coding dependencies between components (such as a direct dependency on a specific database), architects should design the system so that components depend on abstract interfaces. This allows the system to easily swap out implementations (e.g., switching from a SQL database to a NoSQL database) without requiring changes to other components.

Architectural Impact of DIP:

- **Loose Coupling:** Systems designed with DIP are more loosely coupled, making them easier to extend, modify, and test.

- **Testability:** By depending on abstractions, it's easier to mock or stub dependencies in unit tests, improving the system's testability.
- **Flexibility:** The system becomes more flexible, as components can be easily swapped or replaced with minimal impact on the overall architecture.

Design for Change and Scalability

In modern software systems, change is inevitable. As business requirements evolve, user needs shift, and new technologies emerge, software systems must be able to adapt. Designing for change is a critical principle in software architecture, ensuring that systems can grow and evolve without requiring extensive rewrites or introducing instability.

Scalability, on the other hand, refers to the ability of a system to handle increased loads (either in terms of traffic or data) as the system grows. Architects must ensure that systems can scale efficiently, whether by adding more resources (vertical scaling) or distributing the load across multiple nodes (horizontal scaling).

1. Design for Change

To design for change, architects must anticipate future requirements and build flexibility into the system from the start. This involves several key strategies:

Modular Design

A modular system is one in which components are self-contained and independent of one another. This allows changes to be made to one part of the system without affecting other parts. For example, if the business logic for handling payments needs to change, the architecture should allow that change to happen without requiring modifications to the user interface or data storage.

Benefits of Modular Design:

- **Easier Updates:** Changes can be localized to specific modules, reducing the risk of introducing bugs in unrelated parts of the system.
- **Faster Development:** Different teams can work on different modules

independently, speeding up the development process.

- **Improved Maintainability:** Modular systems are easier to maintain, as each module can be tested and updated separately.

Abstraction and Encapsulation

Abstraction involves hiding the implementation details of a component behind a simple interface. This allows the implementation to change without affecting other parts of the system. Encapsulation refers to bundling the data and methods that operate on that data within a single component, protecting the internal state from outside interference.

For example, an API that provides customer data might initially fetch data from a SQL database but later switch to a NoSQL database. By abstracting the data retrieval logic behind a simple interface, the underlying implementation can change without requiring modifications to the rest of the system.

Benefits of Abstraction and Encapsulation:

- **Increased Flexibility:** Components can be easily replaced or updated without affecting other parts of the system.
- **Reduced Complexity:** By hiding the internal workings of a component, abstraction simplifies the system, making it easier to reason about.

Configuration-Driven Design

Configuration-driven design involves separating configuration from code, allowing key settings (such as database connections, feature toggles, or service endpoints) to be modified without changing the underlying code. This is particularly useful in environments where systems need to adapt to different deployment environments or user needs.

For instance, a SaaS application might have different configurations for each client, such as custom branding, workflows, or integrations. By using configuration files or environment variables, these customizations can be applied without modifying the codebase.

Benefits of Configuration-Driven Design:

- **Adaptability:** The system can easily be reconfigured for different environments or use cases.
- **Simplified Updates:** Changes to configuration do not require redeployment or recompilation of the code, making updates faster and less risky.

2. Designing for Scalability

Scalability is a key consideration in software architecture, particularly for systems that need to handle large amounts of

4o

ChatGPT said:

ChatGPT

data or traffic. Architects must ensure that systems are designed to scale efficiently as demand increases. Here are some strategies to consider:

Horizontal vs. Vertical Scaling

Horizontal scaling involves adding more machines or nodes to distribute the load, while vertical scaling involves adding more resources (CPU, RAM) to existing machines. While vertical scaling is easier to implement, it has limits and can be more expensive. Horizontal scaling is often more cost-effective and provides better redundancy.

For example, in a web application, using a load balancer to distribute incoming traffic across multiple web servers allows the system to handle more users simultaneously without overloading a single server.

Benefits of Horizontal Scaling:

- **Increased Resilience:** If one server fails, others can take over, improving the overall reliability of the system.
- **Cost-Effectiveness:** Horizontal scaling often provides a better cost-to-performance ratio compared to vertical scaling.

Caching Strategies

Caching is a powerful technique for improving performance and scalability.

By storing frequently accessed data in memory, systems can reduce the number of database queries and speed up response times. Caches can be implemented at various levels, including database caches, application caches, and content delivery networks (CDNs).

For instance, an e-commerce application might cache product details and user sessions to reduce database load and improve response times for frequently accessed pages.

Benefits of Caching:

- **Improved Performance:** Reducing the load on the database improves response times and overall system performance.
- **Scalability:** Caching allows systems to handle more simultaneous users without requiring additional database resources.

Asynchronous Processing

Asynchronous processing allows systems to handle tasks without blocking the main application flow. By offloading time-consuming operations (such as sending emails, processing payments, or generating reports) to background workers or queues, architects can ensure that the user experience remains responsive.

For example, in an online application, when a user submits a form, the application can immediately acknowledge the submission while processing the request in the background. This approach enhances the user experience by providing immediate feedback.

Benefits of Asynchronous Processing:

- **Improved User Experience:** Users receive quicker feedback, enhancing the overall experience.
- **Better Resource Utilization:** Offloading tasks to background workers allows the system to manage resources more efficiently.

Separation of Concerns and Loose Coupling

Separation of concerns and loose coupling are fundamental principles in software architecture that significantly contribute to the maintainability, scalability, and flexibility of systems.

1. Separation of Concerns

Separation of concerns involves dividing a system into distinct sections, each responsible for a specific aspect of the system's functionality. This principle enhances the clarity and organization of code, making it easier to understand, maintain, and test.

For example, in a typical web application, the responsibilities can be divided into several layers:

- **Presentation Layer:** Manages the user interface and user interactions.
- **Business Logic Layer:** Implements the core functionality and business rules.
- **Data Access Layer:** Handles interactions with data sources, such as databases.

By separating concerns, architects ensure that changes in one area of the system (such as updating the user interface) do not impact other areas (like business logic), reducing complexity and minimizing the risk of introducing bugs.

Benefits of Separation of Concerns:

- **Improved Maintainability:** Each section of the codebase can be modified independently, making it easier to manage changes and updates.
- **Enhanced Clarity:** A well-structured system with clear separation of concerns is easier to understand and navigate, making onboarding new developers faster.
- **Facilitated Testing:** Testing individual components or layers becomes more straightforward when concerns are clearly separated.

2. Loose Coupling

Loose coupling refers to the design of components that are minimally dependent on each other. When components are loosely coupled, changes in one component have little to no impact on other components, making the system more flexible and easier to maintain.

For example, in a microservices architecture, services communicate through well-defined APIs, reducing dependencies. If a service changes its implementation, other services that depend on it remain unaffected as long as the API contract remains the same.

Benefits of Loose Coupling:

- **Flexibility:** Systems can evolve more easily as changes can be made to individual components without affecting the entire system.
- **Reusability:** Loosely coupled components are easier to reuse across different projects or systems.
- **Reduced Complexity:** When components are decoupled, understanding and managing the system becomes easier.

Importance of Maintainability and Testability

Maintainability and testability are critical considerations in software architecture. Systems that are easy to maintain and test save time and resources in the long run, ensuring that they can adapt to changes in requirements or technology.

1. Maintainability

Maintainability refers to how easily a system can be modified to correct defects, improve performance, or adapt to changes in the environment. A maintainable system should allow for straightforward updates and enhancements, reducing the cost and time associated with maintenance.

To enhance maintainability, architects should:

- **Use Clear Naming Conventions:** Consistent and descriptive naming conventions for variables, classes, and methods make it easier for developers to understand the codebase.
- **Document the Architecture:** Comprehensive documentation that outlines the system's architecture, key components, and interactions aids in maintaining the system over time.

- **Implement Coding Standards:** Enforcing coding standards across the team ensures consistency and improves code quality, making it easier to read and maintain.

Benefits of Maintainability:

- **Reduced Costs:** Systems that are easier to maintain incur lower costs over time, as less effort is required to implement changes.
- **Increased Development Speed:** Developers can implement changes more quickly when the system is organized and well-documented.
- **Longer System Lifespan:** Well-maintained systems can adapt to changing requirements and technology, extending their usable life.

2. Testability

Testability refers to how easily a system can be tested to ensure that it behaves as expected. A testable system is designed in such a way that it can be verified through automated tests, unit tests, and integration tests, allowing developers to catch bugs and validate functionality early in the development process.

To improve testability, architects should:

- **Design for Testability:** Components should be designed to allow for easy isolation during testing. This often involves adhering to the Dependency Inversion Principle, allowing for easy mocking of dependencies.
- **Use Automated Testing Tools:** Implementing a robust testing framework that supports automated tests (unit tests, integration tests, and end-to-end tests) improves the reliability of the system.
- **Maintain Clear Interfaces:** Well-defined interfaces make it easier to test components in isolation, enhancing the overall testability of the system.

Benefits of Testability:

- **Increased Confidence in Changes:** With a comprehensive suite of tests, developers can make changes to the codebase with confidence that existing functionality will not be broken.
- **Faster Feedback Loops:** Automated tests provide immediate feedback on the quality of changes, allowing teams to identify and fix issues early in the development process.
- **Improved Collaboration:** When tests are clear and comprehensive, they serve as documentation for expected behavior, improving collaboration among team members.

Conclusion

Architectural principles and best practices are the foundation upon which successful software systems are built. By adhering to the SOLID principles, designing for change and scalability, maintaining separation of concerns and loose coupling, and prioritizing maintainability and testability, architects can create systems that are not only robust and adaptable but also easier to understand and maintain.

In an ever-changing technological landscape, the ability to adapt and evolve is crucial. By embedding these principles into the architecture from the outset, teams can ensure that their systems remain relevant, scalable, and capable of meeting both current and future requirements. As we move forward in this book, we will continue to explore how these principles can be applied to specific architectural patterns and design decisions, further enhancing our understanding of effective software architecture.

Chapter 4: Designing for Change and Scalability

I n the ever-evolving world of software development, the ability to adapt to change and scale effectively is crucial for success. As user demands grow and new technologies emerge, architects must ensure that their systems are designed with flexibility and scalability in mind. This chapter will explore key strategies and best practices for designing software systems that can handle change and scale efficiently, ensuring long-term viability and relevance.

1. Understanding Change in Software Systems

Change is an inevitable part of software development. Whether driven by business requirements, user feedback, or technological advancements, changes can significantly impact a system's architecture. Understanding how to manage change effectively is essential for architects, as it allows them to create systems that can evolve without requiring extensive rewrites or introducing instability.

1.1 Types of Change

Changes to software systems can take various forms, including:

- **Functional Changes:** These involve adding, modifying, or removing features in response to user needs or business goals. For example, a task management tool might need to add a new feature for calendar integration or reporting capabilities.

- **Non-Functional Changes:** These changes affect the performance, security, or usability of the system without altering its functionality. For instance, optimizing a database for better query performance or enhancing security measures are non-functional changes.
- **Technological Changes:** As new technologies emerge, systems may need to adopt new frameworks, libraries, or platforms. For example, transitioning from a monolithic architecture to microservices can significantly impact the overall design and development process.
- **Regulatory Changes:** Compliance with legal or industry standards may necessitate changes in how data is handled, stored, or processed. For example, changes to data privacy laws may require updates to data handling practices.

1.2 The Impact of Change on Software Architecture

Changes in requirements can have far-reaching implications for software architecture. If a system is not designed to accommodate change, the consequences can be detrimental:

- **Increased Technical Debt:** When changes are made without considering the architectural implications, technical debt can accumulate. This debt can hinder future development and lead to a fragile system that is difficult to maintain.
- **Reduced Agility:** A rigid architecture that cannot adapt to change limits an organization's ability to respond to market demands. This lack of agility can result in lost opportunities and competitive disadvantage.
- **Increased Costs:** The cost of implementing changes to a poorly designed system can be significant. This includes the costs of fixing bugs, rewriting code, or even starting over with a new architecture.

2. Strategies for Designing for Change

To create systems that can adapt to change, architects should incorporate several strategies into their design process:

2.1 Modular Design

Modular design is a critical strategy for managing change in software systems. By breaking the system into independent, self-contained modules, architects can ensure that changes in one module do not affect others. This approach promotes flexibility and maintainability, allowing developers to work on different parts of the system simultaneously without conflict.

Benefits of Modular Design:

- **Isolation of Changes:** When changes are needed, they can be made within the affected module without impacting the rest of the system.
- **Ease of Testing:** Individual modules can be tested in isolation, making it easier to identify and fix bugs.
- **Improved Reusability:** Well-designed modules can be reused across different projects or applications, reducing development time.

Implementation of Modular Design:

- **Define Clear Interfaces:** Each module should expose a well-defined interface that other components can interact with. This interface should be stable, even if the internal implementation of the module changes.
- **Use Microservices for Large Applications:** For larger systems, consider adopting a microservices architecture, where each service represents a distinct module with its own responsibilities.

2.2 Abstraction and Encapsulation

Abstraction involves hiding the implementation details of a module behind a simple interface, while encapsulation involves bundling the data and methods that operate on that data within a single component. Together, these principles allow architects to design systems that can evolve without requiring changes to external components.

Benefits of Abstraction and Encapsulation:

- **Flexibility in Implementation:** Changes to the underlying implemen-

43

tation can be made without affecting other parts of the system, as long as the interface remains unchanged.

- **Reduced Complexity:** Abstraction simplifies interactions between components, making the system easier to understand.

Implementation of Abstraction and Encapsulation:

- **Design Interfaces for Components:** Each component should have a well-defined interface that abstracts its functionality. This allows developers to interact with the component without needing to know its internal workings.
- **Use Abstract Classes or Interfaces:** In object-oriented programming, consider using abstract classes or interfaces to define common behaviors for related components.

2.3 Configuration-Driven Design

Configuration-driven design separates configuration from code, allowing key settings (such as feature toggles, database connections, and service endpoints) to be modified without changing the underlying code. This approach enhances the flexibility of the system and makes it easier to adapt to different environments.

Benefits of Configuration-Driven Design:

- **Easy Adaptation:** The system can be quickly adapted for different deployment environments, such as development, testing, and production.
- **Rapid Feature Toggles:** Features can be enabled or disabled through configuration, allowing teams to experiment without changing code.

Implementation of Configuration-Driven Design:

- **External Configuration Files:** Store configuration settings in external files (e.g., JSON, YAML, or XML) that can be easily modified without changing code.

- **Environment Variables:** Use environment variables to manage configuration settings, particularly for sensitive data such as API keys or database credentials.

2.4 Embrace Automation

Automation is a powerful tool for managing change in software systems. By automating repetitive tasks such as testing, deployment, and monitoring, architects can streamline the development process and reduce the risk of human error.

Benefits of Automation:

- **Faster Feedback Loops:** Automated tests provide immediate feedback on code changes, allowing developers to catch bugs early.
- **Consistency in Deployment:** Automation ensures that deployments are consistent across different environments, reducing the risk of issues caused by manual processes.

Implementation of Automation:

- **Continuous Integration/Continuous Deployment (CI/CD):** Implement CI/CD pipelines to automate the process of testing and deploying code changes.
- **Automated Testing Frameworks:** Use automated testing frameworks to validate the functionality of components and ensure that changes do not introduce regressions.

2.5 Agile Methodologies

Adopting agile methodologies can greatly enhance an organization's ability to adapt to change. Agile practices emphasize collaboration, iterative development, and responsiveness to feedback, allowing teams to respond quickly to changing requirements.

Benefits of Agile Methodologies:

- **Increased Flexibility:** Agile teams can quickly pivot based on user feedback or changes in the market.
- **Frequent Releases:** Short development cycles allow teams to deliver value to users more frequently, fostering a culture of continuous improvement.

Implementation of Agile Methodologies:

- **Iterative Development:** Break development into small iterations, focusing on delivering a minimum viable product (MVP) that can be improved based on user feedback.
- **Collaboration and Communication:** Foster open communication between development teams, stakeholders, and users to ensure alignment and quick decision-making.

3. Designing for Scalability

Scalability is the capacity of a system to handle increased load or demand without compromising performance. As businesses grow and user demands increase, architects must ensure that their systems can scale efficiently. Here are key strategies for designing systems with scalability in mind:

3.1 Horizontal vs. Vertical Scaling

Understanding the difference between horizontal and vertical scaling is crucial for designing scalable systems.

Vertical Scaling:

Vertical scaling (or scaling up) involves adding more resources (CPU, RAM, etc.) to an existing machine. While this approach is often simpler to implement, it has limitations and can be costly.

- **Advantages:**
- **Simplicity:** Easier to implement, as it involves upgrading existing hardware.
- **Fewer Changes Required:** No significant architectural changes are needed; existing systems can often benefit from upgraded resources.

- **Disadvantages:**
- **Limits to Growth:** There's a maximum capacity for vertical scaling; eventually, hardware limitations will cap scalability.
- **Costly:** High-performance hardware can be significantly more expensive than commodity hardware used in horizontal scaling.

Horizontal Scaling:

Horizontal scaling (or scaling out) involves adding more machines or instances to distribute the load. This approach is often more cost-effective and offers greater redundancy and fault tolerance.

- **Advantages:**
- **Unlimited Scalability:** Adding more servers allows the system to scale as needed, without hitting resource limits.
- **Fault Tolerance:** If one instance fails, others can take over, improving the system's resilience.
- **Disadvantages:**
- **Complexity:** Implementing horizontal scaling often requires changes to the architecture, such as load balancers and distributed databases.
- **Data Consistency:** Managing data consistency across multiple instances can be challenging, particularly for stateful applications.

Implementation Considerations:

- Assess the application's expected load and growth patterns to determine the most appropriate scaling strategy.
- Design systems that can seamlessly transition from vertical to horizontal scaling, allowing flexibility as requirements change.

3.2 Load Balancing

Load balancing is a technique used to distribute incoming traffic across multiple servers or instances to ensure optimal resource utilization and responsiveness.

Benefits of Load Balancing:

- **Improved Performance:** By distributing requests evenly, load balancing prevents any single server from becoming a bottleneck.
- **High Availability:** If one server goes down, load balancers can reroute traffic to healthy servers, ensuring continuous service.

Implementation Strategies:

- **Hardware Load Balancers:** Dedicated hardware devices that manage traffic distribution across servers.
- **Software Load Balancers:** Use software solutions (e.g., NGINX, HAProxy) to route traffic based on various algorithms (round robin, least connections, etc.).
- **Cloud-Based Load Balancing:** Cloud providers (like AWS and Azure) offer built-in load balancing services that automatically scale based on traffic.

3.3 Caching Strategies

Caching is a technique that stores frequently accessed data in memory, reducing the need to fetch it from slower data sources (such as databases) repeatedly.

Types of Caching:

- **In-Memory Caching:** Store data in memory for fast access (e.g., Redis, Memcached).
- **Database Caching:** Use caching layers to store query results and reduce database load.
- **Content Delivery Networks (CDNs):** Cache static content at various geographical locations to improve access speed for users worldwide.

Benefits of Caching:

- **Increased Performance:** Caching significantly reduces response times, leading to improved user experience.
- **Reduced Load on Databases:** By serving cached data, the system reduces the number of queries hitting the database, improving overall performance.

Implementation Considerations:

- Identify data that is frequently accessed and relatively static, making it a good candidate for caching.
- Implement cache invalidation strategies to ensure that stale data is not served to users. Techniques include time-based expiration, event-driven invalidation, or manual cache purging.

3.4 Asynchronous Processing

Asynchronous processing allows tasks to be executed independently of the main application flow, preventing blocking operations that can slow down the user experience.

Benefits of Asynchronous Processing:

- **Improved Responsiveness:** Users can continue interacting with the application while background tasks are being processed.
- **Better Resource Utilization:** By offloading time-consuming tasks (like data processing or sending emails) to background workers, the application can manage resources more effectively.

Implementation Strategies:

- **Message Queues:** Use message queues (like RabbitMQ or Apache Kafka) to decouple components and enable asynchronous communication between services.
- **Background Workers:** Implement worker processes that listen for tasks in a queue and execute them without blocking the main application.

3.5 Database Scaling

Databases are often a bottleneck in application performance. Architects must design databases with scalability in mind.

Scaling Strategies:

- **Sharding:** Distribute data across multiple database instances, ensuring that no single instance becomes overwhelmed.
- **Replication:** Use master-slave replication to distribute read requests across multiple instances, improving read performance.
- **Database Caching:** Implement caching layers to reduce the load on databases and improve response times.

Benefits of Database Scaling:

- **Increased Throughput:** Scaling databases allows applications to handle higher volumes of transactions without degrading performance.
- **Improved Reliability:** Replication can enhance data availability and fault tolerance.

4. Best Practices for Designing Scalable Systems

Designing scalable systems involves a combination of architectural principles, design patterns, and best practices. Here are some key practices to consider:

4.1 Start with a Solid Architecture

Before building a system, architects should carefully consider the architecture that will support scalability. Starting with a well-defined architecture that incorporates scalability principles allows teams to make informed decisions as the system evolves.

4.2 Prioritize Modularization

Modularization enables teams to build, test, and deploy components independently. This flexibility is critical for scaling applications and adapting to change.

4.3 Monitor and Measure Performance

Implementing monitoring tools allows teams to track system performance in real-time. By measuring key performance indicators (KPIs), architects can identify bottlenecks and make data-driven decisions about scaling.

4.4 Plan for Growth

Architects should anticipate growth and design systems that can scale easily. This involves choosing technologies and patterns that support horizontal scaling and ensuring that the architecture can accommodate future requirements.

4.5 Optimize for Cost

Scalability often involves trade-offs between performance and cost. Architects should design systems that can scale efficiently without incurring excessive costs, leveraging cloud services and automation to optimize resource utilization.

4.6 Implement Automated Testing

Automated testing is critical for maintaining the integrity of the system as it scales. By implementing a comprehensive suite of tests, architects can ensure that changes do not introduce regressions or break existing functionality.

5. Conclusion

Designing for change and scalability is a fundamental aspect of software architecture. As user demands evolve and new technologies emerge, architects must ensure that their systems can adapt without sacrificing performance or maintainability. By embracing modular design, abstraction, configuration-driven design, and automated processes, architects can create systems that are not only robust but also flexible enough to accommodate future growth.

In a landscape where change is constant, the ability to scale efficiently and adapt to new requirements will determine the long-term success of software systems. By adhering to these principles and best practices, architects can build systems that thrive in the face of change, providing value to users and organizations alike. As we move forward in this book, we will continue to explore specific design patterns and architectural choices that further enhance the scalability and adaptability of software systems.

Chapter 5: Architectural Patterns for Scalability and Performance

Scalability and performance are crucial considerations in software architecture. As systems grow and user demands increase, architects must ensure that applications can handle greater loads and maintain optimal performance levels. This chapter will explore various architectural patterns designed to enhance scalability and performance, including microservices architecture, serverless architecture, caching strategies, load balancing, and data partitioning. We will also discuss the advantages and trade-offs associated with each pattern and provide real-world examples to illustrate their applications.

1. Microservices Architecture

1.1 Overview of Microservices Architecture

Microservices architecture is an architectural style that structures an application as a collection of small, independent services, each designed to perform a specific business function. Unlike monolithic architectures, where all components are tightly integrated into a single unit, microservices allow for greater flexibility and scalability.

Each microservice communicates with other services through well-defined APIs, often using lightweight protocols such as HTTP/REST or messaging queues. This separation enables teams to develop, deploy, and scale each service independently, leading to improved agility and faster time-to-market.

1.2 Benefits of Microservices Architecture

- **Scalability:** Microservices can be scaled independently based on demand. For example, if a specific service, like user authentication, experiences high traffic, it can be scaled up without affecting other services.

- **Resilience:** Because each microservice operates independently, a failure in one service does not necessarily bring down the entire system. This improves overall system reliability and availability.

- **Flexibility:** Microservices allow teams to use different technologies and programming languages for different services. This flexibility enables the use of the best tools for each specific task.

- **Faster Development:** Independent teams can work on different microservices simultaneously, speeding up development and enabling continuous integration and deployment.

1.3 Drawbacks of Microservices Architecture

- **Complexity:** Managing a distributed system can introduce significant complexity, particularly in terms of inter-service communication, data consistency, and deployment.

- **Overhead:** Each microservice requires its own infrastructure, which can lead to increased operational overhead in terms of monitoring, maintenance, and resource management.

- **Testing Challenges:** Testing a microservices-based system can be more complex, as it requires testing interactions between multiple services.

1.4 When to Use Microservices Architecture

Microservices architecture is ideal for:

- Large, complex applications that require scalability and flexibility.
- Systems with diverse and evolving requirements that need to be able to integrate new features quickly.

- Organizations with multiple development teams that can work independently on different services.

1.5 Real-World Example: Netflix

Netflix is a prominent example of a company that successfully employs microservices architecture. Originally, Netflix operated as a monolithic application. However, as user demand grew, it transitioned to a microservices architecture to enhance scalability and performance.

- **User Service:** Manages user accounts and profiles.
- **Recommendation Engine:** Provides personalized content suggestions based on user viewing habits.
- **Content Delivery Service:** Responsible for streaming video content to users.
- **Payment Service:** Handles subscription payments and billing.

By adopting microservices, Netflix has achieved the ability to scale individual services based on demand. For instance, during peak usage hours, the content delivery service can be scaled up to accommodate the influx of users while other services remain unaffected.

2. Serverless Architecture

2.1 Overview of Serverless Architecture

Serverless architecture is a cloud computing execution model in which the cloud provider dynamically manages the allocation of machine resources. Developers can deploy functions or applications without worrying about the underlying infrastructure. This allows them to focus solely on writing code.

In a serverless model, applications are built as a collection of small, stateless functions that are executed in response to events or triggers (such as HTTP requests, database changes, or scheduled jobs). The cloud provider automatically scales the resources needed to run these functions based on demand.

2.2 Benefits of Serverless Architecture

- **Cost-Effectiveness:** With serverless architecture, users pay only for the execution time of their functions. This model eliminates costs associated with idle server resources, making it an economical choice for applications with variable workloads.
- **Automatic Scaling:** Serverless architectures automatically scale based on incoming traffic or event triggers. This enables applications to handle sudden spikes in demand without manual intervention.
- **Reduced Operational Overhead:** Developers do not need to manage servers, leading to lower operational complexity and allowing them to focus on writing and deploying code.
- **Rapid Development and Deployment:** Serverless architectures facilitate quick iterations and deployments, enabling teams to deliver features and fixes faster.

2.3 Drawbacks of Serverless Architecture

- **Cold Starts:** Serverless functions may experience latency during cold starts, as the cloud provider needs to provision resources to execute the function. This can impact performance, especially for latency-sensitive applications.
- **Vendor Lock-In:** Serverless architectures often tie applications to specific cloud providers, making it challenging to switch providers or move applications to on-premises environments.
- **Limited Execution Time:** Many serverless platforms impose limits on the execution time of functions, which may not be suitable for long-running tasks.

2.4 When to Use Serverless Architecture
Serverless architecture is ideal for:

- Applications with variable workloads or sporadic usage patterns, such as event-driven applications or APIs.
- Systems that require rapid development and deployment, enabling teams

to iterate quickly.

- Microservices that can be deployed as individual functions responding to specific events.

2.5 Real-World Example: AWS Lambda

AWS Lambda is a popular serverless computing platform that enables developers to run code in response to events without provisioning servers. For example, an image processing application might use AWS Lambda functions to automatically resize images when they are uploaded to an S3 bucket.

- **Event Trigger:** When a user uploads an image to S3, an event triggers the corresponding Lambda function.
- **Processing Logic:** The function processes the image (e.g., resizing, filtering) and saves the results back to S3.
- **Cost Savings:** Users only pay for the execution time of the function, making it a cost-effective solution for image processing.

3. Caching Strategies

3.1 Overview of Caching

Caching is a technique used to store frequently accessed data in memory, reducing the need to fetch it from slower data sources, such as databases or external APIs. By serving cached data, applications can significantly improve response times and reduce load on backend systems.

3.2 Types of Caching

- **In-Memory Caching:** Storing data in memory for fast access. Popular in-memory caching solutions include Redis and Memcached.
- **Database Caching:** Caching results of database queries to minimize load on the database. This can be implemented at the application layer or through database technologies that support caching natively.
- **Content Delivery Networks (CDNs):** Caching static content at edge locations to speed up access for users across different geographical

locations.

3.3 Benefits of Caching

- **Increased Performance:** Caching reduces latency, leading to faster response times for users and improved overall application performance.
- **Reduced Load on Databases:** By serving cached data, applications can significantly reduce the number of database queries, leading to better performance and resource utilization.
- **Enhanced Scalability:** Caching allows applications to handle more concurrent users by reducing the workload on backend systems.

3.4 Implementation Strategies
Identifying Cacheable Data
Determine which data is frequently accessed and relatively static, making it a good candidate for caching. This might include:

- User sessions
- Product details in an e-commerce application
- Static content like images, stylesheets, or scripts

Cache Invalidation Strategies
Implement cache invalidation strategies to ensure that stale data is not served to users. Common strategies include:

- **Time-Based Expiration:** Set a time-to-live (TTL) for cached items, after which they will be automatically invalidated.
- **Event-Driven Invalidation:** Invalidate or refresh cached items in response to specific events, such as updates to the underlying data.

Choosing a Caching Solution
Select the right caching solution based on the application's needs:

- **In-Memory Caches:** For high-speed access to frequently used data.
- **Distributed Caches:** For applications with multiple instances requiring a shared cache.

3.5 Real-World Example: E-Commerce Application Caching

In an e-commerce application, caching can dramatically improve performance:

- **In-Memory Caching for Product Listings:** Product details (such as images, descriptions, and prices) can be cached in memory. When users browse product listings, the application retrieves this data from the cache instead of querying the database, leading to faster load times.
- **User Session Caching:** User session data can be cached to maintain user state between requests, reducing the need for frequent database access.
- **CDN for Static Assets:** By caching images, stylesheets, and scripts on a CDN, the application can serve static assets quickly, reducing latency and improving the user experience.

4. Load Balancing

4.1 Overview of Load Balancing

Load balancing is the process of distributing incoming network traffic across multiple servers or resources to ensure optimal resource utilization, minimize response times, and prevent overload on any single server.

4.2 Benefits of Load Balancing

- **Improved Performance:** By distributing requests evenly across servers, load balancing prevents any single server from becoming a bottleneck, improving overall system performance.
- **High Availability:** Load balancers can reroute traffic in case of server failures, ensuring that users can still access the application without interruption.
- **Scalability:** Load balancing enables horizontal scaling, allowing organizations to add more servers as traffic increases.

4.3 Types of Load Balancers

- **Hardware Load Balancers:** Dedicated hardware devices designed to manage traffic distribution. These can be costly but offer high performance and reliability.
- **Software Load Balancers:** Software solutions (e.g., NGINX, HAProxy) that can be deployed on commodity hardware. These are more flexible and cost-effective.
- **Cloud-Based Load Balancers:** Cloud providers (such as AWS Elastic Load Balancing) offer built-in load balancing services that automatically scale based on traffic.

4.4 Implementation Strategies
Load Balancing Algorithms

Load balancers use algorithms to determine how to distribute incoming traffic. Common algorithms include:

- **Round Robin:** Distributes requests evenly across all servers.
- **Least Connections:** Sends traffic to the server with the fewest active connections.
- **IP Hash:** Routes requests based on the client's IP address, ensuring consistent routing for repeated requests.

Health Checks

Load balancers should implement health checks to monitor the health of servers and ensure that traffic is only sent to healthy instances. If a server fails, the load balancer can reroute traffic to healthy servers automatically.

SSL Termination

Load balancers can offload SSL termination, handling encryption and decryption of traffic. This reduces the load on backend servers and improves performance.

4.5 Real-World Example: Load Balancing in a Web Application

Consider a web application that experiences varying levels of traffic throughout the day. By implementing a load balancer, the application can effectively manage incoming requests:

- **Traffic Distribution:** The load balancer distributes incoming requests across multiple web servers based on the chosen load balancing algorithm, ensuring no single server is overwhelmed.
- **Failover Handling:** If one web server goes down, the load balancer automatically reroutes traffic to healthy servers, maintaining high availability.
- **Scalability:** As traffic increases, new web servers can be added to the pool behind the load balancer, allowing the application to handle more concurrent users without degradation in performance.

5. Data Partitioning
5.1 Overview of Data Partitioning
Data partitioning, also known as sharding, is the practice of dividing a large dataset into smaller, more manageable pieces, known as shards. Each shard can be stored on a separate database or server, allowing for improved performance and scalability.
5.2 Benefits of Data Partitioning

- **Improved Performance:** By distributing data across multiple shards, the system can handle more requests simultaneously, improving response times and overall performance.
- **Scalability:** Data partitioning allows organizations to scale their databases horizontally by adding more shards as the dataset grows.
- **Isolation of Data:** Each shard can be managed independently, making it easier to perform maintenance tasks without impacting the entire system.

5.3 Types of Data Partitioning

- **Horizontal Partitioning:** Also known as sharding, horizontal partitioning involves splitting a table into smaller tables, each containing a subset of the rows. For example, a user database might be partitioned based on user ID ranges.

- **Vertical Partitioning:** In vertical partitioning, a table is divided into smaller tables based on columns. For instance, user profile information could be stored separately from user activity logs.

5.4 Implementation Strategies
Choosing a Partitioning Key

Selecting an appropriate partitioning key is crucial for effective data partitioning. The key should ensure even distribution of data across shards to avoid hotspots (shards that become overloaded while others remain underutilized). Common partitioning keys include:

- **User ID:** Partitioning data based on user ID ranges.
- **Geographic Location:** Partitioning based on geographic regions for applications with a global user base.

Managing Data Consistency

Data consistency can be challenging in a partitioned environment. Architects must implement strategies to maintain consistency across shards, such as:

- **Eventual Consistency:** Allowing for temporary inconsistencies while ensuring that all updates eventually propagate to all shards.
- **Distributed Transactions:** Using distributed transaction protocols (like two-phase commit) to ensure atomicity across multiple shards.

Monitoring and Maintenance

Regular monitoring of shard performance is essential to identify and address imbalances or bottlenecks. Implementing automated processes for shard rebalancing and maintenance can help maintain performance as data grows.

5.5 Real-World Example: Twitter's Data Partitioning

Twitter is a prime example of a company that effectively uses data partitioning to manage its massive user base and tweet volumes:

- **User Data Partitioning:** Twitter partitions user data based on user IDs, distributing users across multiple databases to ensure that no single database becomes a bottleneck.
- **Tweet Storage:** Tweets are also partitioned based on user IDs, allowing for efficient retrieval and storage of tweets associated with individual users.
- **Scalability:** By partitioning data, Twitter can easily add more databases and shards as its user base grows, ensuring that the platform remains responsive even during peak usage times.

6. Best Practices for Scalability and Performance

Designing for scalability and performance requires careful planning and consideration of best practices. Here are some key practices to keep in mind:

6.1 Plan for Growth

Architects should anticipate future growth and design systems that can scale easily. This involves choosing technologies and architectural patterns that support horizontal scaling and ensuring that the architecture can accommodate future requirements.

6.2 Optimize Database Design

A well-designed database is crucial for achieving scalability and performance. Consider implementing techniques such as indexing, normalization, and partitioning to ensure optimal database performance.

6.3 Implement Load Testing

Conducting load testing during the development process allows teams to identify potential bottlenecks and performance issues before the system goes live. Load testing helps ensure that the system can handle expected traffic levels.

6.4 Monitor and Analyze Performance

Implement monitoring tools to track system performance in real-time. By analyzing key performance indicators (KPIs), architects can identify areas for improvement and make data-driven decisions about scaling and optimization.

6.5 Use Content Delivery Networks (CDNs)

For applications that serve static content, implementing a CDN can significantly improve performance by caching content at edge locations closer to users.

6.6 Implement Asynchronous Processing

Asynchronous processing allows applications to handle tasks without blocking the main application flow. Offloading time-consuming operations to background workers or queues can improve responsiveness and resource utilization.

7. Conclusion

Designing for change and scalability is a fundamental aspect of software architecture. By embracing architectural patterns such as microservices, serverless architectures, caching strategies, load balancing, and data partitioning, architects can create systems that not only meet current demands but are also adaptable to future growth.

As user needs evolve and technology advances, the ability to scale efficiently and maintain optimal performance will determine the long-term success of software systems. By adhering to best practices and leveraging the right architectural patterns, teams can build resilient, responsive applications that thrive in an ever-changing landscape.

In the next chapter, we will delve into the importance of security in software architecture, exploring key principles and best practices for designing secure systems that protect user data and maintain trust.

Chapter 6: Ensuring Security in Software Architecture

I n today's digital landscape, security is paramount. With the increasing frequency and sophistication of cyber threats, architects must prioritize security at every stage of the software development lifecycle. This chapter explores essential principles and best practices for designing secure software architectures, covering topics such as threat modeling, secure coding practices, authentication and authorization mechanisms, data protection, and compliance. By implementing robust security measures, organizations can protect their systems, safeguard sensitive data, and maintain user trust.

1. The Importance of Security in Software Architecture

Security in software architecture refers to the design and implementation of systems that are resilient against unauthorized access, attacks, and data breaches. Inadequate security measures can have severe consequences, including financial loss, reputational damage, and legal ramifications. Here are key reasons why security should be a top priority in software architecture:

1.1 Growing Cyber Threats

Cyber threats are on the rise, with attackers employing increasingly sophisticated techniques to exploit vulnerabilities. From data breaches and ransomware attacks to distributed denial-of-service (DDoS) attacks, organizations must proactively defend their systems against a wide range of threats.

1.2 Regulatory Compliance

Many industries are subject to regulations that mandate strict security measures to protect sensitive data. Compliance with standards such as the General Data Protection Regulation (GDPR), Health Insurance Portability and Accountability Act (HIPAA), and Payment Card Industry Data Security Standard (PCI DSS) is essential for avoiding legal penalties and maintaining customer trust.

1.3 Protecting Sensitive Data

Organizations handle vast amounts of sensitive data, including personal information, financial records, and proprietary business information. A data breach can expose this information, leading to significant financial and reputational damage.

1.4 Maintaining User Trust

Users expect organizations to safeguard their data and maintain privacy. Security breaches can erode trust and lead to customer attrition, negatively impacting revenue and brand reputation.

2. Principles of Secure Software Architecture

Designing secure software architectures involves adhering to several key principles that guide architects in building robust, secure systems.

2.1 Least Privilege

The principle of least privilege states that users, systems, and components should only be granted the minimum level of access necessary to perform their functions. By restricting permissions, organizations can minimize the potential attack surface.

Implementation of Least Privilege:

- **Role-Based Access Control (RBAC):** Implement RBAC to define user roles and permissions based on their job functions. For example, an administrator might have access to manage users, while a regular user can only view their own profile.
- **Principle of Separation of Duties:** Divide critical tasks among multiple users to prevent any single individual from having complete control over sensitive processes.

2.2 Defense in Depth

Defense in depth involves layering multiple security measures to protect systems. This approach ensures that if one layer of defense is breached, additional layers remain to thwart the attack.

Implementation of Defense in Depth:

- **Firewalls and Intrusion Detection Systems (IDS):** Use firewalls to control network traffic and IDS to monitor for suspicious activity.
- **Encryption:** Implement encryption to protect sensitive data both in transit and at rest.
- **Multi-Factor Authentication (MFA):** Require multiple forms of verification before granting access to sensitive systems or data.

2.3 Fail-Safe Defaults

Fail-safe defaults, also known as fail-secure, refer to the practice of ensuring that systems are configured to deny access by default. This principle reduces the risk of unauthorized access by requiring explicit permissions for access.

Implementation of Fail-Safe Defaults:

- **Default Deny Policies:** Configure firewalls and access control lists to deny all traffic by default, only allowing traffic from trusted sources or specific protocols.
- **Explicit Permissions:** Require explicit permissions for sensitive actions, such as deleting data or modifying configurations.

2.4 Secure by Design

Secure by design emphasizes incorporating security into the architecture from the beginning rather than as an afterthought. Security should be considered during the design phase, guiding decisions about components, interactions, and technologies.

Implementation of Secure by Design:

- **Threat Modeling:** Conduct threat modeling to identify potential vulnerabilities and design weaknesses before development begins. This helps architects create systems that proactively mitigate risks.

- **Secure Coding Practices:** Adopt secure coding practices to prevent common vulnerabilities such as SQL injection, cross-site scripting (XSS), and buffer overflows.

2.5 Regular Security Audits and Testing

Continuous evaluation of security measures is essential to identify vulnerabilities and ensure that systems remain secure over time. Regular security audits, penetration testing, and code reviews help organizations stay ahead of potential threats.

Implementation of Regular Security Audits:

- **Automated Vulnerability Scanning:** Use automated tools to regularly scan applications for known vulnerabilities and configuration issues.
- **Penetration Testing:** Conduct periodic penetration testing to simulate attacks and identify weaknesses in the system.
- **Security Code Reviews:** Implement security-focused code reviews to catch vulnerabilities early in the development process.

3. Threat Modeling

Threat modeling is a structured approach to identifying and assessing potential threats to a system. By analyzing the system's architecture, data flows, and user interactions, architects can pinpoint vulnerabilities and design strategies to mitigate risks.

3.1 Steps in Threat Modeling

Step 1: Define Security Objectives

Identify the security objectives for the system, such as protecting sensitive data, ensuring availability, and maintaining user privacy. Clearly defining these objectives helps guide the threat modeling process.

Step 2: Create an Architecture Overview

Develop a high-level overview of the system architecture, including components, data flows, and external interactions. This overview serves as the foundation for identifying potential threats.

Step 3: Identify Potential Threats

Analyze the architecture to identify potential threats and vulnerabilities. Common threats to consider include:

- Unauthorized access to sensitive data
- Denial of service (DoS) attacks
- Data breaches or leaks
- Insider threats

Step 4: Assess Risks

Evaluate the likelihood and impact of each identified threat. Consider factors such as the system's sensitivity, potential financial impact, and the ease with which an attacker could exploit the vulnerability.

Step 5: Define Mitigation Strategies

Develop strategies to mitigate identified risks. This may include implementing additional security measures, such as encryption, access controls, or monitoring.

Step 6: Document and Review

Document the threat modeling process, including identified threats, risk assessments, and mitigation strategies. Regularly review and update the threat model as the system evolves or new threats emerge.

3.2 Real-World Example: Threat Modeling for a Web Application

Consider a web application that allows users to submit and manage sensitive information. The threat modeling process might unfold as follows:

1. **Define Security Objectives:** Protect user data, ensure availability, and maintain user privacy.
2. **Create Architecture Overview:** Identify components such as the web server, application server, database, and external APIs.
3. **Identify Potential Threats:** Unauthorized access to user data, SQL injection attacks, session hijacking, and DoS attacks.
4. **Assess Risks:** Determine the likelihood and impact of each threat based

on the application's architecture and user base.

5. **Define Mitigation Strategies:** Implement input validation, prepared statements to prevent SQL injection, use HTTPS for secure data transmission, and apply rate limiting to prevent DoS attacks.

6. **Document and Review:** Document the findings and regularly review the threat model as new features are added.

4. Secure Coding Practices

Secure coding practices are essential for building applications that resist attacks and vulnerabilities. By following established coding standards, developers can minimize the risk of introducing security flaws into the software.

4.1 Input Validation and Sanitization

Input validation involves checking user inputs to ensure they conform to expected formats and constraints. Input sanitization involves cleaning input to remove potentially malicious content.

Best Practices for Input Validation:

- **Whitelist Validation:** Only accept input that matches specific patterns or formats, such as alphanumeric characters for usernames.
- **Length Constraints:** Set limits on the length of user input to prevent buffer overflow attacks.

Best Practices for Input Sanitization:

- **Escape Special Characters:** When displaying user input, escape special characters (e.g., <, >, &, ') to prevent XSS attacks.
- **Strip Dangerous Content:** Remove potentially harmful content, such as HTML tags or script elements, from user input.

4.2 Authentication and Authorization

Robust authentication and authorization mechanisms are crucial for controlling access to sensitive resources. Implementing secure authentication practices helps ensure that only authorized users can access the system.

Best Practices for Authentication:

- **Multi-Factor Authentication (MFA):** Require users to provide additional verification (e.g., SMS code or authenticator app) in addition to their password.
- **Secure Password Storage:** Use strong hashing algorithms (e.g., bcrypt) to securely store passwords, making it difficult for attackers to recover them even if the database is compromised.

Best Practices for Authorization:

- **Role-Based Access Control (RBAC):** Implement RBAC to manage user permissions based on roles, ensuring that users can only access resources necessary for their job functions.
- **Principle of Least Privilege:** Grant users the minimum level of access needed to perform their tasks.

4.3 Error Handling and Logging

Proper error handling and logging practices are essential for maintaining security while providing valuable information for troubleshooting.

Best Practices for Error Handling:

- **Generic Error Messages:** Avoid displaying detailed error messages to users, as they may expose sensitive information about the system.
- **Graceful Degradation:** Implement fallback mechanisms to maintain functionality in the event of an error.

Best Practices for Logging:

- **Log Security Events:** Log security-related events, such as failed login attempts and privilege escalations, to monitor for suspicious activity.
- **Secure Log Storage:** Store logs in a secure location and restrict access

to authorized personnel only.

4.4 Data Protection

Protecting sensitive data is crucial for maintaining user privacy and compliance with regulations. Data protection measures should be implemented throughout the software architecture.

Best Practices for Data Protection:

- **Encryption:** Use encryption to protect sensitive data both in transit and at rest. This ensures that even if data is intercepted, it remains unreadable.
- **Data Masking:** Mask sensitive information in non-production environments to prevent unauthorized access to real data.
- **Access Controls:** Implement strict access controls to restrict access to sensitive data based on user roles and responsibilities.

5. Compliance and Regulatory Considerations

Compliance with regulations and industry standards is a critical aspect of software security. Many organizations are required to adhere to specific security frameworks and guidelines, depending on their industry.

5.1 Common Regulatory Standards

- **General Data Protection Regulation (GDPR):** Regulates the processing of personal data of EU citizens, emphasizing data protection and privacy.
- **Health Insurance Portability and Accountability Act (HIPAA):** Sets standards for protecting sensitive patient information in the healthcare industry.
- **Payment Card Industry Data Security Standard (PCI DSS):** Establishes security requirements for organizations that handle credit card transactions.

5.2 Implementing Compliance Measures
Conduct Regular Audits

Perform regular audits to assess compliance with regulatory requirements and identify potential vulnerabilities.

Training and Awareness

Provide training for employees on security best practices and regulatory requirements to ensure that everyone understands their responsibilities.

Documentation

Maintain comprehensive documentation of security measures, policies, and procedures to demonstrate compliance during audits.

6. Building a Security-First Culture

Creating a security-first culture within an organization is essential for fostering a proactive approach to software security. This involves instilling a mindset that prioritizes security at all levels of development and operations.

6.1 Security Training and Awareness Programs

Implement security training programs to educate employees about the importance of security and best practices for maintaining it. This can include training on secure coding practices, threat awareness, and compliance requirements.

6.2 Integrating Security into the Development Lifecycle

Incorporate security considerations into every stage of the software development lifecycle (SDLC). This includes conducting threat modeling during the design phase, implementing secure coding practices during development, and performing security testing before deployment.

6.3 Encouraging Open Communication

Foster an environment where employees feel comfortable reporting security concerns or vulnerabilities without fear of retribution. Encouraging open communication helps identify and address potential security issues before they escalate.

7. Conclusion

Security in software architecture is a critical consideration that must be prioritized throughout the development lifecycle. By adhering to key principles such as least privilege, defense in depth, fail-safe defaults, and secure by design, architects can build robust, secure systems that protect against a wide range of threats.

Implementing threat modeling, secure coding practices, and effective authentication and authorization mechanisms further enhances the security posture of applications. Additionally, organizations must remain vigilant in the face of evolving cyber threats, ensuring compliance with regulatory requirements and fostering a security-first culture.

As technology continues to evolve, the need for secure software architecture will only grow. By embracing security as an integral part of the design and development process, organizations can build systems that safeguard sensitive data, maintain user trust, and withstand the ever-changing landscape of cyber threats. In the next chapter, we will explore performance optimization techniques to ensure that software systems not only meet security requirements but also deliver exceptional user experiences.

Chapter 7: Performance Optimization Techniques in Software Architecture

P erformance optimization is a critical aspect of software architecture that directly impacts user experience, resource utilization, and overall system effectiveness. As user expectations for speed and responsiveness continue to rise, architects and developers must focus on designing systems that deliver optimal performance under various conditions. This chapter will explore key techniques for optimizing performance in software architecture, covering topics such as profiling and monitoring, caching strategies, load balancing, database optimization, asynchronous processing, and the use of content delivery networks (CDNs). By implementing these strategies, organizations can ensure their applications remain responsive, efficient, and capable of scaling to meet growing demands.

1. Understanding Performance Optimization

Performance optimization involves analyzing and improving the speed, responsiveness, and resource efficiency of software systems. It encompasses various activities, from identifying bottlenecks and inefficiencies to implementing strategies that enhance overall performance.

1.1 Importance of Performance Optimization

Optimizing performance is crucial for several reasons:

- **User Experience:** Users expect applications to respond quickly and efficiently. Delays or sluggish performance can lead to frustration, decreased satisfaction, and increased churn rates.
- **Resource Utilization:** Efficient systems make better use of resources, reducing operational costs and minimizing waste. Performance optimization can lead to lower server costs and reduced energy consumption.
- **Scalability:** As user demand grows, optimized systems are better equipped to handle increased loads without degradation in performance. This scalability is essential for businesses looking to expand their reach.
- **Competitive Advantage:** Organizations that prioritize performance often gain a competitive edge in their markets. Fast and responsive applications attract and retain users, enhancing overall business success.

2. Profiling and Monitoring

2.1 Overview of Profiling and Monitoring

Profiling involves analyzing the performance of an application to identify bottlenecks and areas for improvement. Monitoring refers to continuously tracking system performance in real time, providing insights into application behavior, resource usage, and user interactions.

2.2 Benefits of Profiling and Monitoring

- **Identification of Bottlenecks:** Profiling helps pinpoint slow components or functions that negatively impact performance, enabling targeted optimization efforts.
- **Real-Time Insights:** Monitoring provides ongoing visibility into system performance, allowing teams to respond quickly to performance issues as they arise.
- **Informed Decision-Making:** By analyzing performance data, architects and developers can make informed decisions about resource allocation, scaling strategies, and optimization efforts.

2.3 Tools for Profiling and Monitoring

- **Profiling Tools:** Tools such as JProfiler, VisualVM, and YourKit help developers analyze application performance, memory usage, and execution time of methods and functions.
- **Monitoring Tools:** Solutions like Prometheus, Grafana, New Relic, and Datadog offer real-time monitoring capabilities, providing insights into system performance, user interactions, and resource utilization.

2.4 Best Practices for Profiling and Monitoring

- **Establish Baselines:** Begin by establishing performance baselines to understand normal behavior. This allows teams to identify deviations and performance regressions over time.
- **Monitor Key Metrics:** Focus on monitoring key performance indicators (KPIs) such as response times, throughput, error rates, and resource utilization to gauge application performance effectively.
- **Conduct Regular Profiling:** Regularly profile the application, particularly after significant changes, to ensure that performance remains optimal.

3. Caching Strategies
3.1 Overview of Caching

Caching is a performance optimization technique that involves storing frequently accessed data in memory to reduce the need for expensive operations such as database queries or external API calls. By serving cached data, applications can significantly improve response times and reduce load on backend systems.

3.2 Types of Caching

- **In-Memory Caching:** In-memory caching stores data in the server's memory, allowing for quick access. Popular in-memory caching solutions include Redis and Memcached.
- **Database Caching:** Database caching involves caching query results to minimize load on the database. This can be implemented at the

application layer or through database technologies that support caching natively.

- **Content Delivery Networks (CDNs):** CDNs cache static content (such as images, stylesheets, and scripts) at geographically distributed edge locations, reducing latency for users accessing content from different regions.

3.3 Benefits of Caching

- **Increased Performance:** Caching reduces latency by serving data quickly from memory rather than querying slower data sources.
- **Reduced Load on Databases:** Caching minimizes the number of queries hitting the database, improving overall performance and allowing the database to handle more concurrent users.
- **Enhanced Scalability:** Caching allows applications to handle more users simultaneously by reducing the workload on backend systems.

3.4 Implementation Strategies for Caching
Identifying Cacheable Data
Determine which data is frequently accessed and relatively static, making it a good candidate for caching. Examples of cacheable data include:

- User sessions
- Product details in an e-commerce application
- Static content like images or scripts

Cache Invalidation Strategies
Implement cache invalidation strategies to ensure that stale data is not served to users. Common strategies include:

- **Time-Based Expiration:** Set a time-to-live (TTL) for cached items to automatically invalidate them after a specified duration.
- **Event-Driven Invalidation:** Invalidate or refresh cached items in

response to specific events, such as updates to the underlying data.

Choosing a Caching Solution

Select the right caching solution based on the application's needs:

- **In-Memory Caches:** For high-speed access to frequently used data.
- **Distributed Caches:** For applications with multiple instances requiring a shared cache.

3.5 Real-World Example: E-Commerce Application Caching

In an e-commerce application, caching can dramatically improve performance:

- **In-Memory Caching for Product Listings:** Product details (such as images, descriptions, and prices) can be cached in memory. When users browse product listings, the application retrieves this data from the cache instead of querying the database, leading to faster load times.
- **User Session Caching:** User session data can be cached to maintain user state between requests, reducing the need for frequent database access.
- **CDN for Static Assets:** By caching images, stylesheets, and scripts on a CDN, the application can serve static assets quickly, reducing latency and improving the user experience.

4. Load Balancing

4.1 Overview of Load Balancing

Load balancing is the process of distributing incoming network traffic across multiple servers or resources to ensure optimal resource utilization, minimize response times, and prevent overload on any single server.

4.2 Benefits of Load Balancing

- **Improved Performance:** By distributing requests evenly across servers, load balancing prevents any single server from becoming a bottleneck, improving overall system performance.

- **High Availability:** Load balancers can reroute traffic in case of server failures, ensuring that users can still access the application without interruption.
- **Scalability:** Load balancing enables horizontal scaling, allowing organizations to add more servers as traffic increases.

4.3 Types of Load Balancers

- **Hardware Load Balancers:** Dedicated hardware devices designed to manage traffic distribution. These can be costly but offer high performance and reliability.
- **Software Load Balancers:** Software solutions (e.g., NGINX, HAProxy) that can be deployed on commodity hardware. These are more flexible and cost-effective.
- **Cloud-Based Load Balancers:** Cloud providers (such as AWS Elastic Load Balancing) offer built-in load balancing services that automatically scale based on traffic.

4.4 Implementation Strategies
Load Balancing Algorithms

Load balancers use algorithms to determine how to distribute incoming traffic. Common algorithms include:

- **Round Robin:** Distributes requests evenly across all servers.
- **Least Connections:** Sends traffic to the server with the fewest active connections.
- **IP Hash:** Routes requests based on the client's IP address, ensuring consistent routing for repeated requests.

Health Checks

Load balancers should implement health checks to monitor the health of servers and ensure that traffic is only sent to healthy instances. If a server fails, the load balancer can reroute traffic to healthy servers automatically.

SSL Termination

Load balancers can offload SSL termination, handling encryption and decryption of traffic. This reduces the load on backend servers and improves performance.

4.5 Real-World Example: Load Balancing in a Web Application

Consider a web application that experiences varying levels of traffic throughout the day. By implementing a load balancer, the application can effectively manage incoming requests:

- **Traffic Distribution:** The load balancer distributes incoming requests across multiple web servers based on the chosen load balancing algorithm, ensuring no single server is overwhelmed.
- **Failover Handling:** If one web server goes down, the load balancer automatically reroutes traffic to healthy servers, maintaining high availability.
- **Scalability:** As traffic increases, new web servers can be added to the pool behind the load balancer, allowing the application to handle more concurrent users without degradation in performance.

5. Database Optimization

5.1 Overview of Database Optimization

Database optimization involves implementing techniques to improve the performance of database queries and overall database efficiency. Given that databases are often a bottleneck in application performance, optimizing them is crucial for enhancing scalability and response times.

5.2 Techniques for Database Optimization

1. Indexing

Indexing is a powerful technique that speeds up data retrieval operations. An index is a data structure that improves the speed of data retrieval on a database table.

- **Types of Indexes:**
- **Primary Index:** Automatically created for primary keys.

80

- **Secondary Index:** Created on other columns to speed up queries.
- **Composite Index:** Created on multiple columns for more complex queries.

2. Query Optimization

Optimizing queries can significantly enhance performance. This involves writing efficient SQL queries and using proper joins, filtering, and aggregations.

- **Best Practices for Query Optimization:**
- **Use SELECT statements wisely:** Only select the columns you need instead of using SELECT *.
- **Limit results:** Use LIMIT clauses to restrict the number of returned records when appropriate.
- **Avoid subqueries:** Replace subqueries with JOINs when possible, as JOINs can be more efficient.

3. Normalization and Denormalization

Normalization involves organizing a database to minimize redundancy, while denormalization involves combining tables to improve read performance. Architects must find the right balance between the two based on application needs.

- **Normalization:** Typically, it reduces redundancy, but highly normalized databases may lead to more complex queries.
- **Denormalization:** Can improve performance by reducing the number of joins needed in queries but may increase redundancy.

4. Partitioning

Database partitioning involves dividing a large database into smaller, more manageable pieces. This can improve performance by enabling more efficient data retrieval and management.

- **Horizontal Partitioning (Sharding):** Distributes rows of a table across multiple database instances.
- **Vertical Partitioning:** Distributes columns of a table across multiple tables.

5.3 Real-World Example: Database Optimization in an E-Commerce Application

In an e-commerce application, database optimization techniques can significantly enhance performance:

- **Indexing on Product Searches:** Create indexes on product names and categories to speed up search queries. This ensures that users can quickly find products without long delays.
- **Query Optimization for User Cart:** Use efficient JOINs to retrieve product details for items in the user's cart without excessive subqueries or complex aggregations.
- **Denormalization for Reporting:** For reporting purposes, denormalize data to allow faster access to aggregated sales figures without needing to perform complex joins across multiple tables.

6. Asynchronous Processing

6.1 Overview of Asynchronous Processing

Asynchronous processing allows applications to handle tasks without blocking the main application flow. By offloading time-consuming operations to background workers or queues, applications can remain responsive and improve user experience.

6.2 Benefits of Asynchronous Processing

- **Improved Responsiveness:** Users can continue interacting with the application while background tasks are being processed, leading to a better overall experience.
- **Better Resource Utilization:** Offloading tasks to background workers allows the system to manage resources more effectively, freeing up the

main application to handle user requests.

- **Scalability:** Asynchronous processing can enable systems to scale more effectively, as background tasks can be distributed across multiple workers or servers.

6.3 Implementation Strategies

Message Queues

Use message queues (e.g., RabbitMQ, Apache Kafka) to decouple components and enable asynchronous communication between services. When a user submits a request, the application can place a message in the queue for processing, allowing the user to receive immediate feedback.

Background Workers

Implement worker processes that listen for tasks in a queue and execute them without blocking the main application. This allows for efficient processing of tasks such as sending emails, processing payments, or generating reports.

Event-Driven Architecture

Consider adopting an event-driven architecture, where components communicate through events and respond to changes in real-time. This approach promotes loose coupling and allows for asynchronous processing across services.

6.4 Real-World Example: Asynchronous Processing in a Task Management Application

In a task management application, asynchronous processing can enhance performance:

- **Task Assignment Notifications:** When a task is assigned to a user, the application can enqueue a notification task for processing. The user receives immediate confirmation, while the notification is sent in the background.
- **Report Generation:** When users request reports, the application can generate them asynchronously. Users receive an email notification when the report is ready, allowing them to continue using the application

without waiting.

7. Content Delivery Networks (CDNs)
7.1 Overview of CDNs

A Content Delivery Network (CDN) is a network of distributed servers that cache and deliver content to users based on their geographic location. CDNs enhance the performance and reliability of content delivery by reducing latency and ensuring high availability.

7.2 Benefits of CDNs

- **Reduced Latency:** By caching content at edge locations closer to users, CDNs minimize the distance data must travel, resulting in faster load times.
- **Improved Reliability:** CDNs provide redundancy and failover capabilities, ensuring that content remains accessible even in the event of server failures.
- **Scalability:** CDNs can handle high traffic volumes and sudden spikes in demand without compromising performance.

7.3 Implementing a CDN
Choosing a CDN Provider

Select a CDN provider based on factors such as performance, coverage, pricing, and integration capabilities. Popular CDN providers include Cloudflare, Amazon CloudFront, and Akamai.

Caching Strategies

Implement caching strategies for static assets such as images, stylesheets, and scripts. Configure cache settings to optimize content delivery while ensuring that updates are reflected in a timely manner.

Content Versioning

Use content versioning strategies to manage updates to cached content. This can involve appending version numbers or timestamps to URLs to ensure that users receive the latest content.

7.4 Real-World Example: CDN Implementation in a Media Streaming

Application

In a media streaming application, using a CDN can dramatically improve performance:

- **Video Streaming:** By caching video content on edge servers, the application can deliver content quickly to users, reducing buffering times and enhancing the viewing experience.
- **Static Asset Delivery:** Use a CDN to cache static assets such as images, stylesheets, and JavaScript files, ensuring that users receive these resources quickly from the nearest edge location.

8. Best Practices for Performance Optimization

Optimizing performance requires a combination of architectural principles, design patterns, and best practices. Here are some key practices to consider:

8.1 Start with a Solid Architecture

Before building a system, architects should carefully consider the architecture that will support performance. Starting with a well-defined architecture that incorporates performance principles allows teams to make informed decisions as the system evolves.

8.2 Optimize Database Design

A well-designed database is crucial for achieving performance. Consider implementing techniques such as indexing, normalization, and partitioning to ensure optimal database performance.

8.3 Implement Load Testing

Conducting load testing during the development process allows teams to identify potential bottlenecks and performance issues before the system goes live. Load testing helps ensure that the system can handle expected traffic levels.

8.4 Monitor and Analyze Performance

Implement monitoring tools to track system performance in real-time. By analyzing key performance indicators (KPIs), architects can identify areas for improvement and make data-driven decisions about scaling and optimization.

8.5 Use Content Delivery Networks (CDNs)

For applications that serve static content, implementing a CDN can significantly improve performance by caching content at edge locations closer to users.

8.6 Implement Asynchronous Processing

Asynchronous processing allows applications to handle tasks without blocking the main application flow. Offloading time-consuming operations to background workers or queues can improve responsiveness and resource utilization.

9. Conclusion

Performance optimization is a critical aspect of software architecture that directly impacts user experience, resource utilization, and overall system effectiveness. By implementing key techniques such as profiling and monitoring, caching strategies, load balancing, database optimization, asynchronous processing, and the use of content delivery networks (CDNs), architects can ensure their applications remain responsive, efficient, and capable of scaling to meet growing demands.

In a landscape where user expectations continue to rise, the ability to deliver high-performance applications will determine the long-term success of software systems. By adhering to best practices and leveraging the right architectural patterns, teams can build resilient, responsive applications that thrive in an ever-changing environment.

In the next chapter, we will explore the importance of continuous integration and continuous deployment (CI/CD) practices, examining how they can enhance software quality, streamline development processes, and support rapid iterations.

Chapter 8: Continuous Integration and Continuous Deployment (CI/CD) in Software Architecture

In modern software development, delivering high-quality applications rapidly and reliably is essential. Continuous Integration (CI) and Continuous Deployment (CD) are key practices that enable development teams to achieve this goal. By automating the processes of integration, testing, and deployment, organizations can reduce the time it takes to deliver new features, fixes, and improvements to users. This chapter will delve into the principles and practices of CI/CD, exploring its benefits, tools, implementation strategies, and real-world examples.

1. Understanding Continuous Integration (CI)

1.1 What is Continuous Integration?

Continuous Integration (CI) is a software development practice where developers frequently merge their code changes into a shared repository. Each integration is automatically verified through the use of automated builds and tests. The primary goal of CI is to detect and address integration issues early in the development process, ensuring that the codebase remains stable and that new features can be added without disrupting existing functionality.

1.2 Benefits of Continuous Integration

- **Early Detection of Issues:** Automated tests run with each integration, allowing teams to identify and address bugs early before they become more complex and costly to fix.
- **Improved Code Quality:** Regular integration encourages developers to adhere to coding standards and best practices, leading to a cleaner and more maintainable codebase.
- **Faster Development Cycles:** CI reduces the time required for integration and testing, allowing teams to deliver new features and fixes more quickly.
- **Enhanced Collaboration:** CI promotes collaboration among team members, as they must integrate their changes regularly and communicate about code updates and issues.

1.3 CI Best Practices

To maximize the benefits of CI, development teams should follow best practices, including:

1.3.1 Automate the Build Process

Automate the process of compiling the code and generating executable artifacts. This ensures that the build is consistent and reduces the likelihood of human error.

1.3.2 Run Automated Tests

Implement automated tests to validate the functionality of the application. This should include unit tests, integration tests, and functional tests to ensure comprehensive coverage.

1.3.3 Maintain a Single Source Repository

All code changes should be committed to a single source code repository, facilitating easy access and collaboration among team members.

1.3.4 Keep the Build Fast

Aim for a fast build process, ideally completing within a few minutes. This encourages developers to integrate their changes more frequently and reduces feedback cycles.

1.3.5 Provide Feedback

Ensure that developers receive immediate feedback on the success or failure of their integrations. This can be achieved through notifications, dashboards, or logs.

1.4 Tools for Continuous Integration

Several tools facilitate CI processes, helping teams automate builds, run tests, and provide feedback. Popular CI tools include:

- **Jenkins:** An open-source automation server that supports building, deploying, and automating software projects.
- **CircleCI:** A cloud-based CI tool that provides fast builds and integrates with various version control systems.
- **Travis CI:** A CI service that integrates with GitHub repositories, enabling automated testing and deployment.
- **GitLab CI/CD:** A built-in CI/CD feature of GitLab that allows teams to define pipelines directly within their repositories.

2. Understanding Continuous Deployment (CD)

2.1 What is Continuous Deployment?

Continuous Deployment (CD) is the practice of automatically deploying code changes to production after they have passed automated testing. In a CD pipeline, code is continuously delivered from development to production with minimal manual intervention, enabling teams to release new features, improvements, and fixes quickly and reliably.

2.2 Benefits of Continuous Deployment

- **Faster Time to Market:** CD accelerates the delivery of new features and fixes, allowing organizations to respond quickly to user needs and market demands.
- **Reduced Deployment Risks:** By deploying smaller, incremental changes frequently, teams can minimize the risks associated with large releases and reduce the chances of introducing critical issues.
- **Increased Collaboration:** CD fosters collaboration between development and operations teams, promoting a culture of shared responsibility for the software delivery process.

- **Improved User Feedback:** Continuous deployment enables teams to gather user feedback more quickly, allowing for rapid iterations and improvements based on real-world usage.

2.3 CD Best Practices

To implement effective continuous deployment, teams should adhere to best practices, including:

2.3.1 Automated Deployment Pipelines

Implement automated deployment pipelines that define the steps required to move code from development to production. This ensures consistency and reliability in the deployment process.

2.3.2 Infrastructure as Code (IaC)

Use IaC tools (such as Terraform, Ansible, or CloudFormation) to manage infrastructure changes through code. This approach enables teams to automate the provisioning and configuration of infrastructure, ensuring consistency across environments.

2.3.3 Implement Rollback Mechanisms

Incorporate rollback mechanisms to revert to previous versions of the application quickly in case of deployment failures. This enhances the reliability of the deployment process.

2.3.4 Monitor Production Environments

Implement monitoring and observability tools to track the health and performance of the application in production. This enables teams to identify and address issues quickly.

2.3.5 Ensure Strong Security Practices

Integrate security practices into the CD pipeline, ensuring that security checks are performed before deployment. This can include automated security scanning, vulnerability assessments, and compliance checks.

2.4 Tools for Continuous Deployment

Various tools facilitate the continuous deployment process, helping teams automate deployment and manage infrastructure. Popular CD tools include:

- **Spinnaker:** An open-source continuous delivery platform that enables teams to manage deployments across multiple cloud providers.

- **Argo CD:** A declarative continuous delivery tool for Kubernetes that automates the deployment of applications.
- **Octopus Deploy:** A deployment automation tool that simplifies the process of deploying applications to various environments.
- **AWS CodeDeploy:** A fully managed deployment service that automates application deployments to Amazon EC2 instances and on-premises servers.

3. CI/CD Pipeline Design

3.1 Overview of CI/CD Pipeline

A CI/CD pipeline is a set of automated processes that enable continuous integration, testing, and deployment of code changes. The pipeline consists of multiple stages, each designed to perform specific tasks, from code commits to deployment in production.

3.2 Stages of a CI/CD Pipeline

1. Code Commit

The pipeline begins when developers commit their code changes to the version control system (e.g., Git). Each commit triggers the CI/CD pipeline.

2. Build Stage

In this stage, the code is compiled, and executable artifacts are generated. Automated build tools (like Maven, Gradle, or npm) are used to compile the code and package it for deployment.

3. Automated Testing

Once the build is successful, automated tests are executed to validate the functionality of the application. This typically includes unit tests, integration tests, and functional tests.

4. Deployment to Staging

If all tests pass, the application is deployed to a staging environment, which closely resembles the production environment. This allows for additional testing and validation before deploying to production.

5. User Acceptance Testing (UAT)

In the UAT stage, stakeholders or users test the application in the staging environment to ensure it meets their requirements and expectations.

6. Production Deployment

Once the application has been validated in the staging environment, it is deployed to production. This can be done using a blue-green deployment strategy, canary releases, or rolling updates to minimize downtime and risks.

7. Monitoring and Feedback

After deployment, the application is monitored for performance, errors, and user feedback. Monitoring tools provide insights into application behavior, allowing teams to identify and address issues quickly.

3.3 Example of a CI/CD Pipeline

Consider a web application developed using a microservices architecture. The CI/CD pipeline for this application may look as follows:

1. **Code Commit:** Developers push code changes to the repository.
2. **Build Stage:** The CI tool compiles the code and creates Docker images for each microservice.
3. **Automated Testing:** Unit tests and integration tests are executed for each microservice.
4. **Deployment to Staging:** The Docker images are deployed to a staging environment, where additional functional tests are conducted.
5. **User Acceptance Testing:** Stakeholders perform UAT in the staging environment, providing feedback for any necessary adjustments.
6. **Production Deployment:** The approved microservices are deployed to production using a blue-green deployment strategy.
7. **Monitoring and Feedback:** The application is monitored for performance and user feedback is collected for continuous improvement.

4. Implementing CI/CD in Your Organization

4.1 Assessing Current Processes

Before implementing CI/CD, organizations should assess their current development and deployment processes. Identify existing bottlenecks, challenges, and areas for improvement to inform the CI/CD implementation strategy.

4.2 Define Goals and Objectives

Clearly define the goals and objectives for implementing CI/CD. This may include improving deployment frequency, reducing lead time for changes, increasing the quality of releases, or enhancing collaboration between development and operations teams.

4.3 Choose the Right Tools

Select the appropriate CI/CD tools based on the organization's needs, existing infrastructure, and team expertise. Evaluate tools for CI, CD, testing, monitoring, and version control to create a cohesive toolchain.

4.4 Develop a Pilot Project

Start with a pilot project to implement CI/CD practices in a controlled environment. This allows teams to experiment with processes, identify challenges, and refine their approach before rolling it out to the entire organization.

4.5 Foster a CI/CD Culture

Encourage a culture that embraces CI/CD principles. This involves promoting collaboration between development and operations teams, providing training and resources, and celebrating successes and improvements.

4.6 Continuous Improvement

CI/CD is an ongoing process. Regularly review and refine the CI/CD pipeline based on team feedback, monitoring data, and changing requirements. Foster a culture of continuous improvement to ensure that processes evolve alongside the organization's needs.

5. Challenges and Considerations in CI/CD Implementation

Implementing CI/CD is not without challenges. Organizations must navigate various considerations to ensure successful adoption.

5.1 Cultural Resistance

Transitioning to CI/CD may encounter resistance from team members accustomed to traditional development practices. Addressing concerns and providing training can help ease the transition.

5.2 Tool Overload

With many available tools, organizations may experience tool overload, leading to confusion and inefficiencies. Choose a cohesive set of tools that integrate well and meet the organization's specific needs.

5.3 Legacy Systems

Integrating CI/CD practices with legacy systems can be challenging. Organizations may need to refactor or modernize existing applications to facilitate CI/CD adoption.

5.4 Security Considerations

Integrating security into the CI/CD pipeline is essential. Implement automated security checks and ensure compliance with security best practices throughout the development lifecycle.

6. Real-World Examples of CI/CD Success

Numerous organizations have successfully implemented CI/CD practices to enhance their software development processes. Here are a few notable examples:

6.1 Netflix

Netflix employs CI/CD practices to deliver updates to its streaming platform rapidly. The company has established a robust pipeline that allows teams to deploy code changes multiple times per day. Automated testing and monitoring ensure high-quality releases, while its microservices architecture supports scalability.

6.2 Amazon

Amazon has embraced CI/CD to enable rapid development and deployment across its vast range of services. The company's commitment to automation and agile practices allows it to deliver new features and improvements quickly, providing a seamless experience for its customers.

6.3 Etsy

Etsy has implemented CI/CD practices to enhance its development work-flow and improve collaboration between teams. The company uses automated testing and deployment processes to ensure rapid iterations and maintain a high level of code quality, resulting in a more responsive and reliable platform for users.

7. Conclusion

Continuous Integration and Continuous Deployment (CI/CD) are essential practices in modern software development, enabling teams to deliver high-quality applications rapidly and reliably. By automating the processes of integration, testing, and deployment, organizations can enhance collaboration, reduce time-to-market, and improve overall software quality.

Implementing CI/CD requires careful planning, the right tools, and a culture that embraces continuous improvement. Organizations that prioritize CI/CD practices can position themselves for success in an increasingly competitive digital landscape. As technology continues to evolve, the importance of CI/CD in software architecture will only grow, making it a vital component of any successful development strategy.

In the next chapter, we will explore the role of testing in software architecture, examining different testing strategies, types of tests, and best practices for ensuring software quality throughout the development lifecycle.

Chapter 9: The Role of Testing in Software Architecture

Software testing is a critical component of the software development lifecycle (SDLC) that ensures applications meet quality standards, function as intended, and provide a positive user experience. As applications become more complex, the importance of implementing effective testing strategies in software architecture cannot be overstated. This chapter explores the various types of software testing, their roles in ensuring quality, and best practices for integrating testing into the development process. By emphasizing the significance of testing, organizations can mitigate risks, reduce defects, and deliver high-quality software.

1. Understanding the Importance of Testing

1.1 Defining Software Testing

Software testing is the process of evaluating a software application to identify any discrepancies between the expected and actual outcomes. It involves executing the software to validate its functionality, performance, security, and usability. Testing serves to uncover defects, ensuring that the software meets the requirements outlined in its specifications and is fit for use.

1.2 The Objectives of Software Testing

The primary objectives of software testing include:

- **Defect Detection:** Identifying and rectifying defects in the software before deployment to enhance the overall quality of the product.
- **Verification and Validation:** Ensuring that the software meets specified requirements (verification) and fulfills user needs and expectations (validation).
- **Risk Mitigation:** Reducing the likelihood of failures in production by uncovering potential issues early in the development process.
- **Performance Assurance:** Validating that the software performs well under expected loads and conditions, ensuring a positive user experience.

1.3 The Impact of Testing on Software Quality

Effective testing contributes to overall software quality in several ways:

- **Increased Reliability:** Thorough testing helps ensure that the software performs consistently and reliably in various conditions, leading to greater user trust.
- **Enhanced User Satisfaction:** By delivering a bug-free and performant application, organizations can improve user satisfaction and retention rates.
- **Reduced Maintenance Costs:** Identifying and resolving issues early in the development process can significantly reduce the cost of fixing defects later in the lifecycle.
- **Faster Time-to-Market:** An efficient testing process allows for rapid iterations and releases, enabling organizations to respond quickly to market demands.

2. Types of Software Testing

Software testing can be classified into various categories based on different criteria, including the testing approach, the phase in the development lifecycle, and the purpose of the testing. Below are some of the most common types of software testing.

2.1 Manual Testing

Manual testing involves human testers executing test cases without the assistance of automation tools. Testers manually interact with the application to identify defects and verify functionality.

Advantages of Manual Testing

- **Exploratory Testing:** Testers can explore the application and identify usability issues that automated tests may overlook.
- **Human Insight:** Manual testers can provide valuable feedback on user experience and overall software quality.

Disadvantages of Manual Testing

- **Time-Consuming:** Manual testing can be slower than automated testing, especially for repetitive test cases.
- **Prone to Human Error:** Manual processes are susceptible to mistakes, which can lead to missed defects.

2.2 Automated Testing

Automated testing involves using scripts and tools to execute test cases without human intervention. Automated tests can run quickly and repeatedly, making them ideal for regression testing and scenarios where speed is crucial.

Advantages of Automated Testing

- **Efficiency:** Automated tests can be executed much faster than manual tests, enabling rapid feedback on code changes.
- **Consistency:** Automated tests provide consistent results and can be run multiple times without variation.
- **Reusability:** Once created, automated tests can be reused across different versions of the application.

Disadvantages of Automated Testing

- **Initial Setup Costs:** Developing automated tests requires an investment in tools and resources.
- **Limited Exploration:** Automated tests may not cover edge cases or exploratory testing scenarios effectively.

2.3 Unit Testing

Unit testing focuses on testing individual components or modules of the software in isolation. Unit tests validate the correctness of code logic and ensure that each unit behaves as expected.

Importance of Unit Testing

- **Early Defect Detection:** Unit tests help identify defects at an early stage, reducing the cost of fixing issues later in the development process.
- **Simplifies Debugging:** When a unit test fails, it pinpoints the exact location of the defect, making debugging easier.

2.4 Integration Testing

Integration testing verifies the interaction between different modules or components of the software. This type of testing ensures that the integrated parts work together as intended.

Types of Integration Testing

- **Big Bang Integration:** All components are integrated simultaneously, and testing is performed on the entire system.
- **Incremental Integration:** Components are integrated and tested incrementally, allowing for easier identification of defects.

2.5 Functional Testing

Functional testing evaluates the software against its functional requirements. It ensures that the application behaves as expected and meets the defined specifications.

Types of Functional Testing

- **Smoke Testing:** A preliminary test to check the basic functionality of the application.
- **Regression Testing:** Testing existing functionality to ensure that new changes do not introduce defects.
- **User Acceptance Testing (UAT):** Testing performed by end-users to validate that the software meets their needs.

2.6 Non-Functional Testing

Non-functional testing assesses attributes such as performance, security, usability, and reliability. It evaluates how the application performs under specific conditions rather than its functional behavior.

Types of Non-Functional Testing

- **Performance Testing:** Evaluates the responsiveness, stability, and scalability of the application under various loads.
- **Security Testing:** Identifies vulnerabilities and security weaknesses in the application to ensure data protection.
- **Usability Testing:** Assesses the user interface and overall user experience to ensure that the application is intuitive and easy to use.

2.7 Regression Testing

Regression testing ensures that changes to the codebase, such as new features or bug fixes, do not negatively impact existing functionality. It involves re-running previously executed test cases to validate that the software remains stable.

Importance of Regression Testing

- **Prevents Regressions:** Regular regression testing helps catch issues that may arise from code changes, preventing them from reaching production.
- **Supports Continuous Integration:** Automated regression tests can be integrated into CI pipelines, providing immediate feedback on the impact of changes.

3. Best Practices for Testing in Software Architecture

Implementing effective testing practices is crucial for ensuring software quality. Below are some best practices for integrating testing into software architecture.

3.1 Shift Left Testing

Shift left testing refers to the practice of incorporating testing activities earlier in the software development lifecycle. By prioritizing testing from the initial stages, teams can identify defects sooner and reduce the cost of fixing issues.

Benefits of Shift Left Testing

- **Early Detection of Defects:** Identifying defects early reduces the cost and effort required for remediation.
- **Improved Collaboration:** Developers and testers work closely together, fostering better communication and shared understanding.

3.2 Test Automation

Implementing test automation is essential for improving efficiency and maintaining consistent quality. Automated tests can be executed quickly and reliably, allowing teams to focus on more complex testing scenarios.

Best Practices for Test Automation

- **Identify Test Candidates:** Determine which tests are best suited for automation, such as regression tests, unit tests, and smoke tests.
- **Maintain Test Scripts:** Regularly update and maintain automated test scripts to ensure they remain effective as the application evolves.
- **Use a Testing Framework:** Choose a robust testing framework that aligns with the technology stack and development practices.

3.3 Create a Comprehensive Test Plan

Developing a comprehensive test plan is crucial for ensuring that all aspects of the application are tested thoroughly. A test plan outlines the testing strategy, objectives, scope, resources, and timelines.

Components of a Test Plan

- **Test Objectives:** Define the goals of the testing effort, including functional and non-functional requirements.
- **Scope of Testing:** Outline which features and components will be tested, including any exclusions.
- **Test Environment:** Specify the environments in which testing will take place, including hardware, software, and configurations.
- **Testing Tools:** Identify the tools and frameworks that will be used for testing.

3.4 Conduct Code Reviews

Incorporating code reviews into the development process can help identify potential defects and improve code quality. Peer reviews allow team members to provide feedback and ensure adherence to coding standards and best practices.

Benefits of Code Reviews

- **Early Detection of Issues:** Code reviews can catch defects and vulnerabilities before they become more significant problems.
- **Knowledge Sharing:** Reviews promote knowledge sharing among team members, helping to improve overall team skills.

3.5 Continuous Testing

Continuous testing involves integrating testing into the CI/CD pipeline, ensuring that tests are executed automatically at various stages of the development process. This approach allows teams to receive immediate feedback on the quality of code changes.

Benefits of Continuous Testing

- **Rapid Feedback:** Teams receive quick feedback on the impact of changes, allowing for faster iterations and improvements.
- **Increased Confidence:** Continuous testing enhances confidence in code quality, enabling teams to deploy changes more frequently.

4. Tools for Testing in Software Architecture

Numerous tools and frameworks facilitate the testing process, helping teams automate and streamline their testing efforts. Below are some popular testing tools categorized by their primary purpose.

4.1 Unit Testing Tools

- **JUnit:** A widely used framework for unit testing in Java applications.
- **NUnit:** A testing framework for .NET applications that supports parameterized tests and assertions.
- **pytest:** A powerful testing framework for Python that supports fixtures, parameterized tests, and plugins.

4.2 Functional Testing Tools

- **Selenium:** An open-source tool for automating web browsers, enabling functional testing of web applications.
- **Cypress:** A modern JavaScript-based end-to-end testing framework for web applications.
- **TestComplete:** A commercial functional testing tool that supports a variety of technologies and programming languages.

4.3 Performance Testing Tools

- **Apache JMeter:** An open-source tool for performance testing and load testing of web applications.
- **LoadRunner:** A commercial performance testing tool that simulates virtual users to evaluate application performance under load.
- **Gatling:** An open-source performance testing tool designed for testing web applications, particularly those built with Scala.

4.4 Continuous Integration and Testing Tools

- **Jenkins:** An open-source automation server that supports CI/CD and can integrate with various testing tools.
- **CircleCI:** A cloud-based CI/CD platform that automates testing and deployment workflows.
- **Travis CI:** A CI service that integrates with GitHub repositories and

supports automated testing.

5. Testing Strategies for Different Software Architectures

Different software architectures may require specific testing strategies to ensure quality and performance. Below are testing considerations for various architectural patterns.

5.1 Monolithic Architecture

In a monolithic architecture, all components of the application are tightly integrated into a single codebase. Testing strategies for monolithic applications include:

- **End-to-End Testing:** Perform comprehensive testing of the entire application to validate that all components work together seamlessly.
- **Integration Testing:** Focus on testing interactions between various modules within the monolith to ensure they function correctly together.

5.2 Microservices Architecture

In a microservices architecture, applications are composed of independent services that communicate through APIs. Testing strategies for microservices include:

- **Service Contract Testing:** Validate that each microservice adheres to its API contract, ensuring compatibility with other services.
- **End-to-End Testing:** Conduct end-to-end tests that simulate user scenarios involving multiple microservices to validate their interactions.
- **Consumer-Driven Contracts:** Implement consumer-driven contract testing to ensure that changes in a service do not break consumers relying on that service.

5.3 Serverless Architecture

In a serverless architecture, applications are built using functions that are executed in response to events. Testing strategies for serverless applications include:

- **Function Testing:** Test individual serverless functions in isolation to ensure they perform their designated tasks correctly.
- **Integration Testing:** Validate interactions between functions and other services, such as databases or APIs, to ensure smooth communication.

6. Challenges in Software Testing

While testing is essential for ensuring software quality, it also presents various challenges. Addressing these challenges effectively can lead to improved testing practices.

6.1 Complexity of Applications

As applications grow in complexity, testing them becomes more challenging. The interplay between various components, dependencies, and technologies can introduce risks and increase the difficulty of thorough testing.

6.2 Resource Constraints

Limited resources, including time, budget, and personnel, can hinder testing efforts. Organizations may struggle to allocate sufficient resources for comprehensive testing, leading to potential gaps in coverage.

6.3 Rapid Development Cycles

In Agile and CI/CD environments, the rapid pace of development can make it challenging to maintain thorough testing practices. Teams must balance speed with quality, ensuring that testing remains a priority amidst tight deadlines.

6.4 Evolving Requirements

Changing requirements can complicate testing efforts, as teams may need to adapt test cases and strategies based on new functionality or shifts in priorities. Maintaining alignment between testing and evolving requirements is crucial.

7. Conclusion

Testing is a fundamental aspect of software architecture that ensures quality, reliability, and performance. By implementing effective testing strategies, organizations can identify defects early, reduce risks, and deliver high-quality software to users.

As software systems become increasingly complex, the role of testing in the development process will only grow. By adopting best practices, leveraging the right tools, and fostering a culture of quality, organizations can enhance their testing efforts and build software that meets user needs and expectations.

In the next chapter, we will explore the importance of documentation in software architecture, examining how comprehensive documentation practices contribute to project success, facilitate collaboration, and ensure knowledge transfer within development teams.

Chapter 10: Documentation in Software Architecture

Documentation plays a crucial role in the success of software architecture. It serves as a reference guide for developers, stakeholders, and users, providing essential information about the system's design, functionality, and operational processes. Effective documentation facilitates communication, supports collaboration, and ensures that knowledge is preserved throughout the software development lifecycle (SDLC). This chapter will explore the importance of documentation in software architecture, the different types of documentation, best practices for creating effective documentation, and the tools available to support documentation efforts.

1. Understanding the Importance of Documentation

1.1 Defining Software Documentation

Software documentation encompasses all written materials that describe the design, functionality, and use of software systems. This includes technical documentation, user manuals, system architecture diagrams, API documentation, and more. Effective documentation provides a clear understanding of the software's purpose, structure, and behavior.

1.2 Objectives of Software Documentation

The primary objectives of software documentation include:

- **Communication:** Documentation serves as a communication tool between developers, stakeholders, and users. It conveys critical information about the software system and its components.
- **Knowledge Transfer:** Documentation preserves knowledge about the system, enabling new team members to onboard quickly and reducing reliance on individual expertise.
- **Reference Material:** Documentation acts as a reference for developers, providing guidance on implementation details, design decisions, and coding standards.
- **Quality Assurance:** Well-documented systems facilitate testing and validation, ensuring that the software meets its requirements and functions as intended.

1.3 The Impact of Documentation on Software Quality

Effective documentation contributes to overall software quality in several ways:

- **Reduced Errors:** Clear and concise documentation helps prevent misunderstandings and miscommunications, reducing the likelihood of errors during development.
- **Enhanced Collaboration:** Documentation fosters collaboration among team members, allowing them to align on project goals, architecture, and implementation strategies.
- **Improved Maintainability:** Comprehensive documentation makes it easier to maintain and update software systems, ensuring that changes can be implemented smoothly.
- **Increased User Satisfaction:** User documentation provides valuable information about the software, enhancing the user experience and

satisfaction.

2. Types of Software Documentation

Software documentation can be classified into various categories based on its purpose and audience. Below are some common types of documentation relevant to software architecture.

2.1 Technical Documentation

Technical documentation provides detailed information about the software system, including architecture, design decisions, and implementation details. It is primarily intended for developers and technical stakeholders.

Key Components of Technical Documentation

- **System Architecture Diagrams:** Visual representations of the system's architecture, illustrating components, relationships, and interactions.
- **Design Specifications:** Detailed descriptions of the software's design, including data models, algorithms, and interfaces.
- **Code Documentation:** Comments and annotations within the codebase that explain the purpose and functionality of specific code segments.

2.2 User Documentation

User documentation is designed to assist end-users in understanding and effectively using the software. It provides guidance on features, functionality, and troubleshooting.

Key Components of User Documentation

- **User Manuals:** Comprehensive guides that outline how to use the software, including step-by-step instructions and examples.
- **FAQs:** A compilation of frequently asked questions and answers to address common user concerns.

- **Tutorials and How-To Guides:** Practical guides that provide users with hands-on instructions for performing specific tasks within the software.

2.3 API Documentation

API documentation describes the application's programming interface, detailing how developers can interact with the software through APIs. It is essential for third-party developers and internal teams that need to integrate with the system.
   Key Components of API Documentation

- **Endpoint Descriptions:** Detailed information about API endpoints, including their purpose, parameters, and expected responses.
- **Examples:** Code snippets and examples that demonstrate how to use the API effectively.
- **Authentication and Authorization:** Information on how to authenticate requests and manage access to the API.

2.4 Process Documentation

Process documentation outlines the processes and workflows involved in the software development lifecycle. It serves as a guide for teams to follow best practices and maintain consistency.
   Key Components of Process Documentation

- **Development Methodologies:** Descriptions of the methodologies used (e.g., Agile, Scrum, Waterfall) and how they are applied in the organization.
- **Version Control Procedures:** Guidelines for using version control systems (e.g., Git) and managing code changes.
- **Testing Processes:** Documentation of testing strategies, including types of tests, testing environments, and reporting procedures.

3. Best Practices for Effective Documentation

Creating effective documentation requires careful planning, organization, and attention to detail. Below are best practices to ensure that documentation is useful and valuable.

3.1 Define Clear Objectives

Before creating documentation, define clear objectives regarding its purpose and audience. Understand what information needs to be conveyed and who will be using the documentation. This clarity will guide the content and structure of the documentation.

3.2 Use Consistent Terminology

Consistency in terminology is essential for clarity. Establish a glossary of terms and ensure that the same terminology is used throughout the documentation. This reduces confusion and helps users understand concepts more easily.

3.3 Organize Documentation Effectively

Organize documentation logically, grouping related content together. Use clear headings, subheadings, and bullet points to break up text and make it easier to read. A well-structured document enhances usability and allows users to find information quickly.

3.4 Include Visual Aids

Incorporate visual aids such as diagrams, flowcharts, and screenshots to complement textual information. Visual representations can enhance understanding and retention, especially for complex concepts.

3.5 Keep Documentation Up-to-Date

Regularly review and update documentation to reflect changes in the software, architecture, or processes. Outdated documentation can lead to confusion and errors, so it's essential to maintain accuracy.

3.6 Solicit Feedback

Encourage feedback from users and stakeholders regarding the documentation. Use this feedback to identify areas for improvement and make adjustments as necessary. Engaging users in the documentation process ensures that it meets their needs.

4. Tools for Documentation

Various tools can facilitate the documentation process, helping teams create, organize, and maintain documentation efficiently. Below are some popular documentation tools categorized by their primary purpose.

4.1 Documentation Generators

- **Doxygen:** A documentation generator for C++, C, Java, and other programming languages. It generates documentation from annotated source code.
- **Sphinx:** A documentation generator for Python projects that can produce HTML, LaTeX, and PDF outputs. It is often used for creating technical documentation.
- **MkDocs:** A static site generator for building project documentation using Markdown. It is user-friendly and easy to set up.

4.2 Wiki and Collaboration Tools

- **Confluence:** A collaboration tool that allows teams to create, organize, and share documentation in a wiki-style format.
- **MediaWiki:** The software behind Wikipedia, MediaWiki is an open-source wiki platform that enables collaborative documentation.
- **Notion:** A versatile tool for creating notes, documentation, and project management, allowing teams to organize information flexibly.

4.3 Version Control for Documentation

- **Git:** A widely used version control system that allows teams to manage documentation alongside code changes. Markdown files can be stored in Git repositories for easy tracking and collaboration.
- **GitHub Pages:** A feature of GitHub that allows users to host documentation websites directly from GitHub repositories, making it easy to publish and share documentation.

4.4 API Documentation Tools

- **Swagger/OpenAPI:** A framework for designing, documenting, and consuming RESTful APIs. It allows developers to create interactive API documentation that can be tested directly from the documentation interface.
- **Postman:** A collaboration platform for API development that provides tools for testing APIs and generating documentation.

5. Integrating Documentation into the Development Process

Incorporating documentation into the software development process is essential for ensuring that documentation remains relevant and up-to-date. Below are strategies for effectively integrating documentation into the SDLC.

5.1 Agile Documentation Practices

In Agile development, documentation should be lightweight and adaptive. Instead of creating extensive documentation upfront, teams can adopt the following practices:

- **Just-In-Time Documentation:** Document features and decisions as they are implemented rather than waiting until the end of the project.
- **Collaborative Documentation:** Encourage collaboration among team members to create and maintain documentation collectively.
- **User Stories and Acceptance Criteria:** Incorporate documentation into user stories and acceptance criteria, ensuring that requirements are clear and well-defined.

5.2 Continuous Documentation

Continuous documentation refers to the practice of updating documentation as changes occur in the codebase. This can be achieved through:

- **Integrating Documentation into CI/CD Pipelines:** Automate the generation of documentation as part of the CI/CD pipeline, ensuring that documentation is always current with the latest code changes.
- **Versioning Documentation:** Use version control to track changes to documentation alongside code changes, allowing teams to manage updates effectively.

5.3 Documentation Reviews

Conduct regular documentation reviews to ensure that documentation remains accurate and relevant. This can involve:

- **Peer Reviews:** Encourage team members to review each other's documentation to provide feedback and identify areas for improvement.

- **Stakeholder Reviews:** Involve stakeholders in reviewing documentation to ensure that it meets their needs and expectations.

6. Challenges in Software Documentation

While documentation is essential for software architecture, it also presents challenges that organizations must address. Below are some common challenges in software documentation.

6.1 Keeping Documentation Up-to-Date

Maintaining accurate and current documentation can be a challenge, especially in fast-paced development environments. Regular updates and reviews are necessary to ensure that documentation reflects the latest changes.

6.2 Balancing Detail and Clarity

Finding the right balance between providing sufficient detail and maintaining clarity can be difficult. Documentation that is too verbose may overwhelm users, while overly concise documentation may lack essential information.

6.3 Resistance to Documentation

Team members may resist creating and maintaining documentation due to time constraints or a lack of perceived value. Encouraging a culture that values documentation is essential for overcoming this resistance.

6.4 Fragmentation of Documentation

Documentation may become fragmented if different teams or individuals create it independently without coordination. Establishing clear guidelines and a centralized repository can help mitigate this issue.

7. Conclusion

Documentation is a vital component of software architecture that significantly impacts the success of software projects. By providing clear, comprehensive, and up-to-date information, documentation facilitates communication, knowledge transfer, and collaboration among developers, stakeholders, and users.

Effective documentation practices, including defining clear objectives, maintaining consistency, and integrating documentation into the development process, can enhance software quality and improve the overall user experience. By leveraging the right tools and strategies, organizations can create documentation that adds value and supports their software development efforts.

As software systems continue to evolve, the importance of documentation will only grow. By prioritizing documentation as an integral part of the software architecture, organizations can ensure that they build resilient, maintainable, and user-friendly applications.

In the next chapter, we will explore the future of software architecture, examining emerging trends, technologies, and best practices that will shape the landscape of software development in the years to come.

Chapter 11: The Future of Software Architecture

As technology continues to evolve at an unprecedented pace, software architecture is undergoing significant transformations. The advent of new tools, methodologies, and paradigms is reshaping how applications are designed, developed, and deployed. This chapter explores the future of software architecture, examining emerging trends, technologies, and best practices that are likely to influence the software development landscape. By understanding these trends, organizations can better prepare for the challenges and opportunities that lie ahead.

1. The Shift Toward Cloud-Native Architecture

1.1 What is Cloud-Native Architecture?

Cloud-native architecture refers to the design and development of applications that are built to leverage cloud computing principles. Cloud-native applications are typically designed to be scalable, resilient, and flexible, taking full advantage of the benefits offered by cloud environments.

1.2 Key Characteristics of Cloud-Native Architecture

- **Microservices:** Cloud-native applications are often built using a microservices architecture, where applications are composed of small, independently deployable services that communicate over APIs.
- **Containerization:** Containers (e.g., Docker) are used to package applications and their dependencies, ensuring consistency across environments and simplifying deployment.
- **Dynamic Orchestration:** Orchestration tools (e.g., Kubernetes) manage the deployment, scaling, and operation of containerized applications, automating many operational tasks.
- **Resilience and Fault Tolerance:** Cloud-native applications are designed to handle failures gracefully, using techniques such as redundancy, auto-scaling, and circuit breakers.

1.3 Benefits of Cloud-Native Architecture

- **Scalability:** Cloud-native applications can scale horizontally, allowing organizations to handle increased loads without compromising performance.
- **Agility:** The use of microservices and containers enables rapid development and deployment cycles, allowing teams to iterate quickly and respond to changing business needs.
- **Cost Efficiency:** By leveraging cloud resources, organizations can optimize resource utilization and reduce infrastructure costs.
- **Improved Collaboration:** Cloud-native architecture promotes collaboration among development and operations teams, facilitating a DevOps culture.

2. Embracing DevOps and Continuous Delivery

2.1 Understanding DevOps

DevOps is a cultural and professional movement that emphasizes collaboration between development and operations teams. It aims to shorten the development lifecycle and improve the quality of software through automation, continuous integration, and continuous delivery (CI/CD).

2.2 The Role of DevOps in Software Architecture

DevOps practices influence software architecture in several ways:

- **Integration of Development and Operations:** DevOps fosters collaboration between teams, leading to more streamlined development and deployment processes.
- **Automation of Testing and Deployment:** Automated testing and deployment pipelines are integral to DevOps, ensuring that code changes are verified and delivered quickly.
- **Monitoring and Feedback Loops:** Continuous monitoring and feedback help teams identify issues early and make data-driven decisions to improve software quality.

2.3 Benefits of DevOps in Software Architecture

- **Faster Time to Market:** DevOps practices enable organizations to release software more quickly and respond to market demands promptly.
- **Higher Quality Software:** By integrating testing and monitoring into the development process, teams can identify and address defects earlier, resulting in higher-quality software.
- **Increased Efficiency:** Automation of repetitive tasks frees up team members to focus on more strategic initiatives, improving overall productivity.

3. The Rise of Serverless Architecture

3.1 What is Serverless Architecture?

Serverless architecture is a cloud computing model where the cloud provider manages the infrastructure and automatically allocates resources as needed. Developers write and deploy functions that are executed in response to events, without the need to manage servers.

3.2 Key Characteristics of Serverless Architecture

- **Event-Driven:** Serverless applications are often triggered by events such as HTTP requests, file uploads, or database changes.
- **Automatic Scaling:** The cloud provider automatically scales resources based on demand, allowing applications to handle varying workloads seamlessly.
- **Pay-As-You-Go Pricing:** Organizations only pay for the compute time consumed by their functions, eliminating costs associated with idle resources.

3.3 Benefits of Serverless Architecture

- **Reduced Operational Overhead:** Developers can focus on writing code without worrying about server management and maintenance.
- **Cost Efficiency:** Pay-as-you-go pricing allows organizations to optimize costs, particularly for applications with variable workloads.
- **Faster Time to Market:** The simplicity of serverless architecture enables rapid development and deployment cycles.

3.4 Use Cases for Serverless Architecture

- **Microservices:** Serverless functions can be used to implement microservices that respond to events and perform specific tasks.
- **Data Processing:** Serverless architecture is well-suited for data processing tasks, such as real-time analytics and batch processing.
- **API Backends:** Serverless functions can serve as lightweight backends for APIs, handling requests and returning responses quickly.

4. The Emergence of Artificial Intelligence (AI) and Machine Learning (ML)

4.1 The Impact of AI and ML on Software Architecture

Artificial Intelligence (AI) and Machine Learning (ML) are transforming how applications are designed and developed. These technologies enable software to learn from data, make predictions, and automate decision-making processes.

4.2 Key Considerations for AI and ML in Software Architecture

- **Data Management:** AI and ML applications rely on large volumes of data. Designing an architecture that supports data collection, storage, and processing is essential.
- **Model Deployment:** The architecture must accommodate the deployment of trained ML models, allowing them to be integrated into applications seamlessly.
- **Scalability:** AI and ML workloads can be resource-intensive. Ensuring that the architecture can scale to meet demand is critical for performance.

4.3 Benefits of Integrating AI and ML into Software Architecture

- **Enhanced User Experience:** AI-powered applications can provide personalized recommendations, improve search functionality, and automate customer support.
- **Improved Decision-Making:** Organizations can leverage data-driven insights to make informed decisions and optimize business processes.
- **Automation of Repetitive Tasks:** AI and ML can automate mundane tasks, allowing teams to focus on higher-value activities.

4.4 Use Cases for AI and ML in Software Architecture

- **Predictive Analytics:** Applications that analyze historical data to predict future trends or behaviors.
- **Natural Language Processing (NLP):** Applications that process and understand human language, such as chatbots and virtual assistants.
- **Computer Vision:** Applications that analyze and interpret visual data, enabling use cases like image recognition and facial detection.

5. Emphasizing Security in Software Architecture

5.1 The Growing Importance of Security

As cyber threats become more sophisticated, security must be a top priority in software architecture. Organizations need to build security into the software development lifecycle to protect sensitive data and maintain user trust.

5.2 Security by Design

Security by design involves integrating security practices into every stage of the software development process. This proactive approach helps identify and mitigate vulnerabilities early in the lifecycle.

5.3 Key Considerations for Security in Software Architecture

- **Threat Modeling:** Conducting threat modeling sessions to identify potential vulnerabilities and attack vectors.
- **Secure Coding Practices:** Implementing secure coding standards to prevent common vulnerabilities, such as SQL injection and cross-site scripting (XSS).
- **Automated Security Testing:** Incorporating automated security testing tools into the CI/CD pipeline to identify vulnerabilities before deployment.

5.4 Benefits of Emphasizing Security

- **Reduced Risk of Breaches:** Proactive security measures can significantly lower the likelihood of data breaches and cyberattacks.
- **Enhanced Compliance:** Organizations can better meet regulatory requirements and avoid legal penalties by prioritizing security.
- **Increased User Trust:** Demonstrating a commitment to security can enhance user confidence and loyalty.

6. Embracing Agile and Lean Principles

6.1 The Agile Manifesto

The Agile Manifesto outlines principles for agile software development, emphasizing collaboration, flexibility, and customer satisfaction. Agile methodologies prioritize iterative development and continuous feedback.

6.2 Lean Principles in Software Development

Lean principles focus on minimizing waste and maximizing value. By adopting lean practices, organizations can streamline development processes, reduce cycle times, and enhance overall efficiency.

6.3 Benefits of Agile and Lean Practices

- **Improved Flexibility:** Agile and lean practices allow teams to adapt to changing requirements and market conditions quickly.
- **Faster Delivery:** Iterative development and continuous feedback enable organizations to release software more frequently and respond to user needs.
- **Enhanced Collaboration:** Agile methodologies promote collaboration among team members and stakeholders, fostering a culture of shared responsibility.

6.4 Integrating Agile and Lean into Software Architecture

To effectively integrate agile and lean practices into software architecture, organizations should:

- **Emphasize Collaboration:** Foster a culture of collaboration between development, operations, and other stakeholders.
- **Adopt Iterative Design:** Implement iterative design processes that allow for continuous improvement based on user feedback.
- **Focus on Value Delivery:** Prioritize features and functionalities that deliver the most value to users.

7. The Role of Open Source in Software Architecture

7.1 The Open Source Movement

The open-source movement advocates for the free distribution and modification of software. Open-source software encourages collaboration and innovation, allowing developers to build upon existing solutions.

7.2 Benefits of Open Source in Software Architecture

- **Cost Savings:** Open-source solutions are often free to use, reducing licensing costs for organizations.
- **Community Support:** Open-source projects benefit from community-driven support, with developers collaborating to improve and maintain the software.
- **Flexibility and Customization:** Organizations can customize open-source solutions to meet their specific needs and requirements.

7.3 Popular Open Source Tools for Software Architecture

- **Kubernetes:** An open-source container orchestration platform that simplifies the deployment, scaling, and management of containerized applications.
- **Apache Kafka:** An open-source distributed streaming platform that enables organizations to build real-time data pipelines and streaming applications.
- **TensorFlow:** An open-source machine learning framework that provides tools for building and deploying AI and ML applications.

7.4 Challenges of Open Source in Software Architecture

While open-source solutions offer numerous benefits, organizations must also consider potential challenges, including:

- **Licensing Issues:** Understanding and complying with open-source licenses is essential to avoid legal issues.
- **Maintenance and Support:** Organizations may need to allocate resources to maintain and support open-source solutions.
- **Security Risks:** Open-source software can be vulnerable to security risks if not properly maintained and updated.

8. Preparing for the Future

8.1 Continuous Learning and Adaptation

As the software landscape evolves, organizations must foster a culture of continuous learning and adaptation. This involves:

- **Investing in Training:** Providing team members with opportunities to learn new technologies, methodologies, and best practices.
- **Encouraging Innovation:** Creating an environment that encourages experimentation and innovation, allowing teams to explore new ideas and solutions.

8.2 Embracing Emerging Technologies

Organizations should stay informed about emerging technologies that may impact software architecture, including:

- **Quantum Computing:** Exploring the potential of quantum computing to solve complex problems and enhance computational power.
- **Edge Computing:** Leveraging edge computing to process data closer to the source, reducing latency and improving performance for IoT applications.
- **5G Technology:** Adopting 5G technology to enable faster communication and enhanced capabilities for mobile and IoT applications.

8.3 Building Resilience

Building resilient software architectures is essential for navigating an increasingly complex and unpredictable environment. Strategies for resilience include:

- **Redundancy and Failover:** Implementing redundancy and failover mechanisms to ensure availability in the event of failures.

- **Monitoring and Observability:** Utilizing monitoring tools to gain insights into application performance and identify issues proactively.
- **Scalability and Flexibility:** Designing architectures that can scale horizontally and adapt to changing demands.

9. Conclusion

The future of software architecture is marked by rapid technological advancements, evolving methodologies, and a growing emphasis on quality, security, and collaboration. By embracing cloud-native architectures, DevOps practices, serverless computing, AI and ML integration, and agile principles, organizations can build resilient, scalable, and high-quality software systems.

As the software landscape continues to evolve, the importance of documentation, testing, and collaboration will remain paramount. Organizations that prioritize continuous learning, innovation, and adaptability will be better positioned to thrive in an increasingly competitive environment.

In this rapidly changing world, software architects must remain vigilant and proactive, continuously seeking opportunities to improve and enhance their architectural practices. By doing so, they can create software systems that not only meet the needs of today's users but also anticipate the challenges and opportunities of tomorrow.

As we move forward, the principles and best practices outlined in this chapter will serve as a foundation for building the next generation of software architectures, paving the way for innovation and success in an ever-evolving digital landscape.

Chapter 12: Testing Strategies for Software Architecture

Testing is a critical aspect of software architecture that ensures applications function as intended, meet quality standards, and provide a positive user experience. As software systems become increasingly complex, implementing effective testing strategies is essential for identifying defects, validating functionality, and mitigating risks. This chapter delves into the various testing strategies applicable to software architecture, exploring the different types of tests, methodologies, and best practices that can enhance software quality. By adopting a comprehensive testing approach, organizations can deliver reliable, high-performing applications that meet user expectations.

1. The Importance of Testing in Software Architecture

1.1 Defining Software Testing

Software testing is the process of evaluating and verifying that a software application or system meets the specified requirements and functions correctly. It involves executing the software to identify defects, assess performance, and validate functionality. Effective testing is essential for ensuring that software is reliable, secure, and usable.

1.2 Objectives of Software Testing

The primary objectives of software testing include:

- **Defect Detection:** Identifying and addressing defects in the software before deployment to enhance the overall quality of the product.
- **Verification and Validation:** Ensuring that the software meets specified requirements (verification) and fulfills user needs and expectations (validation).
- **Risk Mitigation:** Reducing the likelihood of failures in production by uncovering potential issues early in the development process.
- **Performance Assurance:** Validating that the software performs well under expected loads and conditions, ensuring a positive user experience.

1.3 The Impact of Testing on Software Quality

Effective testing contributes to overall software quality in several ways:

- **Increased Reliability:** Thorough testing helps ensure that the software performs consistently and reliably in various conditions, leading to greater user trust.
- **Enhanced User Satisfaction:** By delivering a bug-free and performant application, organizations can improve user satisfaction and retention rates.
- **Reduced Maintenance Costs:** Identifying and resolving issues early in the development process can significantly reduce the cost of fixing defects later in the lifecycle.
- **Faster Time-to-Market:** An efficient testing process allows for rapid iterations and releases, enabling organizations to respond quickly to market demands.

2. Types of Software Testing

Software testing can be classified into various categories based on different criteria, including the testing approach, the phase in the development lifecycle, and the purpose of the testing. Below are some of the most common types of software testing.

2.1 Manual Testing

Manual testing involves human testers executing test cases without the assistance of automation tools. Testers manually interact with the application to identify defects and verify functionality.

Advantages of Manual Testing

- **Exploratory Testing:** Testers can explore the application and identify usability issues that automated tests may overlook.
- **Human Insight:** Manual testers can provide valuable feedback on user experience and overall software quality.

Disadvantages of Manual Testing

- **Time-Consuming:** Manual testing can be slower than automated testing, especially for repetitive test cases.
- **Prone to Human Error:** Manual processes are susceptible to mistakes, which can lead to missed defects.

2.2 Automated Testing

Automated testing involves using scripts and tools to execute test cases without human intervention. Automated tests can run quickly and repeatedly, making them ideal for regression testing and scenarios where speed is crucial.

Advantages of Automated Testing

- **Efficiency:** Automated tests can be executed much faster than manual tests, enabling rapid feedback on code changes.
- **Consistency:** Automated tests provide consistent results and can be run multiple times without variation.
- **Reusability:** Once created, automated tests can be reused across different versions of the application.

Disadvantages of Automated Testing

- **Initial Setup Costs:** Developing automated tests requires an investment in tools and resources.
- **Limited Exploration:** Automated tests may not cover edge cases or exploratory testing scenarios effectively.

2.3 Unit Testing

Unit testing focuses on testing individual components or modules of the software in isolation. Unit tests validate the correctness of code logic and ensure that each unit behaves as expected.

Importance of Unit Testing

- **Early Defect Detection:** Unit tests help identify defects at an early stage, reducing the cost of fixing issues later in the development process.
- **Simplifies Debugging:** When a unit test fails, it pinpoints the exact location of the defect, making debugging easier.

2.4 Integration Testing

Integration testing verifies the interaction between different modules or components of the software. This type of testing ensures that the integrated parts work together as intended.

Types of Integration Testing

- **Big Bang Integration:** All components are integrated simultaneously, and testing is performed on the entire system.
- **Incremental Integration:** Components are integrated and tested incrementally, allowing for easier identification of defects.

2.5 Functional Testing

Functional testing evaluates the software against its functional requirements. It ensures that the application behaves as expected and meets the defined specifications.

Types of Functional Testing

- **Smoke Testing:** A preliminary test to check the basic functionality of the application.
- **Regression Testing:** Testing existing functionality to ensure that new changes do not introduce defects.
- **User Acceptance Testing (UAT):** Testing performed by end-users to validate that the software meets their needs.

2.6 Non-Functional Testing

Non-functional testing assesses attributes such as performance, security, usability, and reliability. It evaluates how the application performs under specific conditions rather than its functional behavior.

Types of Non-Functional Testing

- **Performance Testing:** Evaluates the responsiveness, stability, and scalability of the application under various loads.
- **Security Testing:** Identifies vulnerabilities and security weaknesses in the application to ensure data protection.
- **Usability Testing:** Assesses the user interface and overall user experience to ensure that the application is intuitive and easy to use.

2.7 Regression Testing

Regression testing ensures that changes to the codebase, such as new features or bug fixes, do not negatively impact existing functionality. It involves re-running previously executed test cases to validate that the software remains stable.

Importance of Regression Testing

- **Prevents Regressions:** Regular regression testing helps catch issues that may arise from code changes, preventing them from reaching production.
- **Supports Continuous Integration:** Automated regression tests can be integrated into CI pipelines, providing immediate feedback on the impact of changes.

3. Best Practices for Testing in Software Architecture

Implementing effective testing practices is crucial for ensuring software quality. Below are some best practices for integrating testing into software architecture.

3.1 Shift Left Testing

Shift left testing refers to the practice of incorporating testing activities earlier in the software development lifecycle. By prioritizing testing from the initial stages, teams can identify defects sooner and reduce the cost of fixing issues.

Benefits of Shift Left Testing

- **Early Detection of Defects:** Identifying defects early reduces the cost and effort required for remediation.
- **Improved Collaboration:** Developers and testers work closely together, fostering better communication and shared understanding.

3.2 Test Automation

Implementing test automation is essential for improving efficiency and maintaining consistent quality. Automated tests can be executed quickly and reliably, allowing teams to focus on more complex testing scenarios.

Best Practices for Test Automation

- **Identify Test Candidates:** Determine which tests are best suited for automation, such as regression tests, unit tests, and smoke tests.
- **Maintain Test Scripts:** Regularly update and maintain automated test scripts to ensure they remain effective as the application evolves.
- **Use a Testing Framework:** Choose a robust testing framework that aligns with the technology stack and development practices.

3.3 Create a Comprehensive Test Plan

Developing a comprehensive test plan is crucial for ensuring that all aspects of the application are tested thoroughly. A test plan outlines the testing strategy, objectives, scope, resources, and timelines.

Components of a Test Plan

- **Test Objectives:** Define the goals of the testing effort, including functional and non-functional requirements.
- **Scope of Testing:** Outline which features and components will be tested, including any exclusions.
- **Test Environment:** Specify the environments in which testing will take place, including hardware, software, and configurations.
- **Testing Tools:** Identify the tools and frameworks that will be used for testing.

3.4 Conduct Code Reviews

Incorporating code reviews into the development process can help identify potential defects and improve code quality. Peer reviews allow team members to provide feedback and ensure adherence to coding standards and best practices.

Benefits of Code Reviews

- **Early Detection of Issues:** Code reviews can catch defects and vulnerabilities before they become more significant problems.
- **Knowledge Sharing:** Reviews promote knowledge sharing among team members, helping to improve overall team skills.

3.5 Continuous Testing

Continuous testing involves integrating testing into the CI/CD pipeline, ensuring that tests are executed automatically at various stages of the development process. This approach allows teams to receive immediate feedback on the quality of code changes.

Benefits of Continuous Testing

- **Rapid Feedback:** Teams receive quick feedback on the impact of changes, allowing for faster iterations and improvements.
- **Increased Confidence:** Continuous testing enhances confidence in code quality, enabling teams to deploy changes more frequently.

4. Tools for Testing in Software Architecture

Numerous tools and frameworks facilitate the testing process, helping teams automate and streamline their testing efforts. Below are some popular testing tools categorized by their primary purpose.

4.1 Unit Testing Tools

- **JUnit:** A widely used framework for unit testing in Java applications.
- **NUnit:** A testing framework for .NET applications that supports parameterized tests and assertions.
- **pytest:** A powerful testing framework for Python that supports fixtures, parameterized tests, and plugins.

4.2 Functional Testing Tools

- **Selenium:** An open-source tool for automating web browsers, enabling functional testing of web applications.
- **Cypress:** A modern JavaScript-based end-to-end testing framework for web applications.
- **TestComplete:** A commercial functional testing tool that supports a variety of technologies and programming languages.

4.3 Performance Testing Tools

- **Apache JMeter:** An open-source tool for performance testing and load testing of web applications.
- **LoadRunner:** A commercial performance testing tool that simulates virtual users to evaluate application performance under load.
- **Gatling:** An open-source performance testing tool designed for testing web applications, particularly those built with Scala.

4.4 Continuous Integration and Testing Tools

- **Jenkins:** An open-source automation server that supports CI/CD and can integrate with various testing tools.
- **CircleCI:** A cloud-based CI/CD platform that automates testing and deployment workflows.
- **Travis CI:** A CI service that integrates with GitHub repositories and

supports automated testing.

5. Testing Strategies for Different Software Architectures

Different software architectures may require specific testing strategies to ensure quality and performance. Below are testing considerations for various architectural patterns.

5.1 Monolithic Architecture

In a monolithic architecture, all components of the application are tightly integrated into a single codebase. Testing strategies for monolithic applications include:

- **End-to-End Testing:** Perform comprehensive testing of the entire application to validate that all components work together seamlessly.
- **Integration Testing:** Focus on testing interactions between various modules within the monolith to ensure they function correctly together.

5.2 Microservices Architecture

In a microservices architecture, applications are composed of independent services that communicate through APIs. Testing strategies for microservices include:

- **Service Contract Testing:** Validate that each microservice adheres to its API contract, ensuring compatibility with other services.
- **End-to-End Testing:** Conduct end-to-end tests that simulate user scenarios involving multiple microservices to validate their interactions.
- **Consumer-Driven Contracts:** Implement consumer-driven contract testing to ensure that changes in a service do not break consumers relying on that service.

5.3 Serverless Architecture

In a serverless architecture, applications are built using functions that are executed in response to events. Testing strategies for serverless applications include:

- **Function Testing:** Test individual serverless functions in isolation to ensure they perform their designated tasks correctly.
- **Integration Testing:** Validate interactions between functions and other services, such as databases or APIs, to ensure smooth communication.

6. Challenges in Software Testing

While testing is essential for ensuring software quality, it also presents various challenges. Addressing these challenges effectively can lead to improved testing practices.

6.1 Complexity of Applications

As applications grow in complexity, testing them becomes more challenging. The interplay between various components, dependencies, and technologies can introduce risks and increase the difficulty of thorough testing.

6.2 Resource Constraints

Limited resources, including time, budget, and personnel, can hinder testing efforts. Organizations may struggle to allocate sufficient resources for comprehensive testing, leading to potential gaps in coverage.

6.3 Rapid Development Cycles

In Agile and CI/CD environments, the rapid pace of development can make it challenging to maintain thorough testing practices. Teams must balance speed with quality, ensuring that testing remains a priority amidst tight deadlines.

6.4 Evolving Requirements

Changing requirements can complicate testing efforts, as teams may need to adapt test cases and strategies based on new functionality or shifts in priorities. Maintaining alignment between testing and evolving requirements is crucial.

7. Conclusion

Testing is a fundamental aspect of software architecture that ensures quality, reliability, and performance. By implementing effective testing strategies, organizations can identify defects early, reduce risks, and deliver high-quality software to users.

As software systems become increasingly complex, the role of testing in the development process will only grow. By adopting best practices, leveraging the right tools, and fostering a culture of quality, organizations can enhance their testing efforts and build software that meets user needs and expectations.

In this rapidly changing world, software architects must remain vigilant and proactive, continuously seeking opportunities to improve and enhance their architectural practices. By doing so, they can create software systems that not only meet the needs of today's users but also anticipate the challenges and opportunities of tomorrow.

As we move forward, the principles and best practices outlined in this chapter will serve as a foundation for building the next generation of software architectures, paving the way for innovation and success in an ever-evolving digital landscape.

In the next chapter, we will explore the role of documentation in software architecture, examining how comprehensive documentation practices contribute to project success, facilitate collaboration, and ensure knowledge transfer within development teams.

Chapter 13: The Role of Documentation in Software Architecture

D
ocumentation is a critical pillar of successful software architecture. It serves as a reference point for developers, stakeholders, and users, providing essential insights into the design, functionality, and operational procedures of software systems. Effective documentation fosters collaboration, supports knowledge transfer, and ensures the longevity and maintainability of applications. In this chapter, we will explore the significance of documentation in software architecture, the various types of documentation, best practices for creating impactful documentation, and the tools that facilitate documentation efforts.

1. The Importance of Documentation in Software Architecture

1.1 Defining Software Documentation

Software documentation encompasses all written materials that describe a software application's design, functionality, usage, and maintenance. This includes technical specifications, user manuals, architecture diagrams, API documentation, and process guides. Effective documentation provides clarity and understanding for all stakeholders involved in the software development lifecycle.

1.2 Objectives of Software Documentation

The primary objectives of software documentation include:

- **Facilitating Communication:** Documentation serves as a communication tool among developers, stakeholders, and users, ensuring everyone is aligned and informed about the system's features and requirements.
- **Supporting Knowledge Transfer:** Documentation preserves critical knowledge about the software architecture, allowing new team members to onboard quickly and reducing reliance on individual expertise.
- **Providing Reference Material:** Documentation acts as a reference guide for developers, offering guidance on implementation details, design decisions, and coding standards.
- **Ensuring Quality Assurance:** Well-documented systems facilitate testing and validation, ensuring that the software meets its requirements and functions as intended.

1.3 The Impact of Documentation on Software Quality

Effective documentation contributes to overall software quality in several ways:

- **Reduced Errors:** Clear and concise documentation helps prevent misunderstandings and miscommunications, reducing the likelihood of errors during development.
- **Enhanced Collaboration:** Documentation fosters collaboration among team members, allowing them to align on project goals, architecture, and implementation strategies.
- **Improved Maintainability:** Comprehensive documentation makes it easier to maintain and update software systems, ensuring that changes can be implemented smoothly.
- **Increased User Satisfaction:** User documentation provides valuable information about the software, enhancing the user experience and

satisfaction.

2. Types of Software Documentation

Software documentation can be categorized into various types based on its purpose and audience. Below are some common types of documentation relevant to software architecture.

2.1 Technical Documentation

Technical documentation provides detailed information about the software system, including architecture, design decisions, and implementation details. It is primarily intended for developers and technical stakeholders.

Key Components of Technical Documentation

- **System Architecture Diagrams:** Visual representations of the system's architecture, illustrating components, relationships, and interactions.
- **Design Specifications:** Detailed descriptions of the software's design, including data models, algorithms, and interfaces.
- **Code Documentation:** Comments and annotations within the codebase that explain the purpose and functionality of specific code segments.

2.2 User Documentation

User documentation is designed to assist end-users in understanding and effectively using the software. It provides guidance on features, functionality, and troubleshooting.

Key Components of User Documentation

- **User Manuals:** Comprehensive guides that outline how to use the software, including step-by-step instructions and examples.
- **FAQs:** A compilation of frequently asked questions and answers to address common user concerns.

- **Tutorials and How-To Guides:** Practical guides that provide users with hands-on instructions for performing specific tasks within the software.

2.3 API Documentation

API documentation describes the application's programming interface, detailing how developers can interact with the software through APIs. It is essential for third-party developers and internal teams that need to integrate with the system.

Key Components of API Documentation

- **Endpoint Descriptions:** Detailed information about API endpoints, including their purpose, parameters, and expected responses.
- **Examples:** Code snippets and examples that demonstrate how to use the API effectively.
- **Authentication and Authorization:** Information on how to authenticate requests and manage access to the API.

2.4 Process Documentation

Process documentation outlines the processes and workflows involved in the software development lifecycle. It serves as a guide for teams to follow best practices and maintain consistency.

Key Components of Process Documentation

- **Development Methodologies:** Descriptions of the methodologies used (e.g., Agile, Scrum, Waterfall) and how they are applied in the organization.
- **Version Control Procedures:** Guidelines for using version control systems (e.g., Git) and managing code changes.
- **Testing Processes:** Documentation of testing strategies, including types of tests, testing environments, and reporting procedures.

3. Best Practices for Effective Documentation

Creating effective documentation requires careful planning, organization, and attention to detail. Below are best practices to ensure that documentation is useful and valuable.

3.1 Define Clear Objectives

Before creating documentation, define clear objectives regarding its purpose and audience. Understand what information needs to be conveyed and who will be using the documentation. This clarity will guide the content and structure of the documentation.

3.2 Use Consistent Terminology

Consistency in terminology is essential for clarity. Establish a glossary of terms and ensure that the same terminology is used throughout the documentation. This reduces confusion and helps users understand concepts more easily.

3.3 Organize Documentation Effectively

Organize documentation logically, grouping related content together. Use clear headings, subheadings, and bullet points to break up text and make it easier to read. A well-structured document enhances usability and allows users to find information quickly.

3.4 Include Visual Aids

Incorporate visual aids such as diagrams, flowcharts, and screenshots to complement textual information. Visual representations can enhance understanding and retention, especially for complex concepts.

3.5 Keep Documentation Up-to-Date

Regularly review and update documentation to reflect changes in the software, architecture, or processes. Outdated documentation can lead to confusion and errors, so it's essential to maintain accuracy.

3.6 Solicit Feedback

Encourage feedback from users and stakeholders regarding the documentation. Use this feedback to identify areas for improvement and make adjustments as necessary. Engaging users in the documentation process ensures that it meets their needs.

4. Tools for Documentation

Various tools can facilitate the documentation process, helping teams create, organize, and maintain documentation efficiently. Below are some popular documentation tools categorized by their primary purpose.

4.1 Documentation Generators

- **Doxygen:** A documentation generator for C++, C, Java, and other programming languages. It generates documentation from annotated source code.
- **Sphinx:** A documentation generator for Python projects that can produce HTML, LaTeX, and PDF outputs. It is often used for creating technical documentation.
- **MkDocs:** A static site generator for building project documentation using Markdown. It is user-friendly and easy to set up.

4.2 Wiki and Collaboration Tools

- **Confluence:** A collaboration tool that allows teams to create, organize, and share documentation in a wiki-style format.
- **MediaWiki:** The software behind Wikipedia, MediaWiki is an open-source wiki platform that enables collaborative documentation.
- **Notion:** A versatile tool for creating notes, documentation, and project management, allowing teams to organize information flexibly.

4.3 Version Control for Documentation

- **Git:** A widely used version control system that allows teams to manage documentation alongside code changes. Markdown files can be stored in Git repositories for easy tracking and collaboration.
- **GitHub Pages:** A feature of GitHub that allows users to host documentation websites directly from GitHub repositories, making it easy to publish and share documentation.

4.4 API Documentation Tools

- **Swagger/OpenAPI:** A framework for designing, documenting, and consuming RESTful APIs. It allows developers to create interactive API documentation that can be tested directly from the documentation interface.
- **Postman:** A collaboration platform for API development that provides tools for testing APIs and generating documentation.

5. Integrating Documentation into the Development Process

Incorporating documentation into the software development process is essential for ensuring that documentation remains relevant and up-to-date. Below are strategies for effectively integrating documentation into the SDLC.

5.1 Agile Documentation Practices

In Agile development, documentation should be lightweight and adaptive. Instead of creating extensive documentation upfront, teams can adopt the following practices:

- **Just-In-Time Documentation:** Document features and decisions as they are implemented rather than waiting until the end of the project.
- **Collaborative Documentation:** Encourage collaboration among team members to create and maintain documentation collectively.
- **User Stories and Acceptance Criteria:** Incorporate documentation into user stories and acceptance criteria, ensuring that requirements are clear and well-defined.

5.2 Continuous Documentation

Continuous documentation refers to the practice of updating documentation as changes occur in the codebase. This can be achieved through:

- **Integrating Documentation into CI/CD Pipelines:** Automate the generation of documentation as part of the CI/CD pipeline, ensuring that documentation is always current with the latest code changes.
- **Versioning Documentation:** Use version control to track changes to documentation alongside code changes, allowing teams to manage updates effectively.

5.3 Documentation Reviews

Conduct regular documentation reviews to ensure that documentation remains accurate and relevant. This can involve:

- **Peer Reviews:** Encourage team members to review each other's documentation to provide feedback and identify areas for improvement.

- **Stakeholder Reviews:** Involve stakeholders in reviewing documentation to ensure that it meets their needs and expectations.

6. Challenges in Software Documentation

While documentation is essential for software architecture, it also presents challenges that organizations must address. Below are some common challenges in software documentation.

6.1 Keeping Documentation Up-to-Date

Maintaining accurate and current documentation can be a challenge, especially in fast-paced development environments. Regular updates and reviews are necessary to ensure that documentation reflects the latest changes.

6.2 Balancing Detail and Clarity

Finding the right balance between providing sufficient detail and maintaining clarity can be difficult. Documentation that is too verbose may overwhelm users, while overly concise documentation may lack essential information.

6.3 Resistance to Documentation

Team members may resist creating and maintaining documentation due to time constraints or a lack of perceived value. Encouraging a culture that values documentation is essential for overcoming this resistance.

6.4 Fragmentation of Documentation

Documentation may become fragmented if different teams or individuals create it independently without coordination. Establishing clear guidelines and a centralized repository can help mitigate this issue.

7. Conclusion

Documentation is a vital component of software architecture that significantly impacts the success of software projects. By providing clear, comprehensive, and up-to-date information, documentation facilitates communication, knowledge transfer, and collaboration among developers, stakeholders, and users.

Effective documentation practices, including defining clear objectives, maintaining consistency, and integrating documentation into the development process, can enhance software quality and improve the overall user experience. By leveraging the right tools and strategies, organizations can create documentation that adds value and supports their software development efforts.

As software systems continue to evolve, the importance of documentation will only grow. By prioritizing documentation as an integral part of the software architecture, organizations can ensure that they build resilient, maintainable, and user-friendly applications.

In the next chapter, we will explore the future of software architecture, examining emerging trends, technologies, and best practices that will shape the landscape of software development in the years to come.

Chapter 14: Emerging Trends and Technologies in Software Architecture

The landscape of software architecture is rapidly evolving, influenced by advancements in technology, changing business requirements, and the increasing complexity of software systems. As organizations strive to remain competitive and responsive to market demands, understanding emerging trends and technologies is essential for software architects and developers. This chapter explores the key trends shaping the future of software architecture, including cloud-native development, microservices, serverless architecture, AI and machine learning, containerization, edge computing, and more. By examining these trends, organizations can better prepare for the challenges and opportunities that lie ahead.

1. Cloud-Native Development

1.1 Defining Cloud-Native Development

Cloud-native development refers to building applications that are designed to leverage the advantages of cloud computing. This approach focuses on creating applications that are scalable, resilient, and adaptable to the dynamic nature of cloud environments. Cloud-native applications are typically built using microservices architecture and are optimized for deployment in cloud platforms.

1.2 Key Characteristics of Cloud-Native Applications

- **Microservices Architecture:** Cloud-native applications are composed of small, independent services that communicate via APIs. This modular approach allows for greater flexibility and scalability.
- **Containerization:** Containers (e.g., Docker) package applications and their dependencies, ensuring consistency across different environments and simplifying deployment.
- **Dynamic Orchestration:** Tools like Kubernetes automate the deployment, scaling, and management of containerized applications, optimizing resource utilization.
- **Resilience and Fault Tolerance:** Cloud-native applications are designed to handle failures gracefully, using techniques such as circuit breakers and redundancy.

1.3 Benefits of Cloud-Native Development

- **Scalability:** Cloud-native applications can scale horizontally, allowing organizations to handle increased traffic without compromising performance.
- **Agility:** The use of microservices and containers enables rapid development and deployment cycles, allowing teams to iterate quickly and respond to changing business needs.
- **Cost Efficiency:** By leveraging cloud resources, organizations can optimize resource utilization and reduce infrastructure costs.
- **Improved Collaboration:** Cloud-native development fosters collaboration between development and operations teams, promoting a DevOps culture.

1.4 Case Study: Cloud-Native Adoption

A notable example of cloud-native development is **Netflix**, which has embraced cloud-native principles to deliver its streaming service. By leveraging microservices architecture, Netflix can rapidly deploy new features and scale its infrastructure to meet fluctuating demand. The company uses **AWS** as its cloud provider, enabling it to focus on development while relying on cloud resources for scalability and resilience.

2. Microservices Architecture

2.1 Understanding Microservices

Microservices architecture is an architectural style that structures an application as a collection of small, loosely coupled services. Each microservice is responsible for a specific business capability and can be developed, deployed, and scaled independently.

2.2 Key Principles of Microservices

- **Independence:** Each microservice can be developed and deployed independently, allowing teams to work on different services simultaneously.
- **Single Responsibility:** Each microservice is designed to perform a specific function, adhering to the principle of single responsibility.
- **Decentralized Data Management:** Microservices can manage their own data, allowing teams to choose the best database technology for each service.
- **Inter-Service Communication:** Microservices communicate through APIs, often using lightweight protocols such as HTTP/REST or messaging queues.

2.3 Benefits of Microservices Architecture

- **Scalability:** Organizations can scale individual microservices based on demand, optimizing resource utilization and performance.
- **Flexibility:** Teams can use different technologies and programming languages for each microservice, enabling greater innovation and experimentation.
- **Resilience:** The failure of one microservice does not affect the entire application, enhancing overall system resilience.
- **Faster Time to Market:** Microservices enable teams to deliver new features and updates more quickly, improving responsiveness to market demands.

2.4 Challenges of Microservices Architecture

- **Complexity:** Managing a distributed system of microservices can introduce complexity, requiring robust monitoring and management tools.
- **Data Consistency:** Ensuring data consistency across microservices can be challenging, particularly in systems with multiple data stores.
- **Deployment and Monitoring:** Organizations need to implement effective deployment strategies and monitoring solutions to manage microservices effectively.

3. Serverless Architecture

3.1 Defining Serverless Architecture

Serverless architecture is a cloud computing model where the cloud provider manages the infrastructure and automatically allocates resources as needed. Developers write and deploy functions that are executed in response to events, without the need to manage servers.

3.2 Key Characteristics of Serverless Architecture

- **Event-Driven:** Serverless applications are triggered by events such as HTTP requests, file uploads, or database changes.
- **Automatic Scaling:** The cloud provider automatically scales resources based on demand, allowing applications to handle varying workloads seamlessly.
- **Pay-As-You-Go Pricing:** Organizations only pay for the compute time consumed by their functions, eliminating costs associated with idle resources.

3.3 Benefits of Serverless Architecture

- **Reduced Operational Overhead:** Developers can focus on writing code without worrying about server management and maintenance.
- **Cost Efficiency:** Pay-as-you-go pricing allows organizations to optimize costs, particularly for applications with variable workloads.
- **Faster Time to Market:** The simplicity of serverless architecture enables rapid development and deployment cycles.

3.4 Use Cases for Serverless Architecture

- **Microservices:** Serverless functions can be used to implement microservices that respond to events and perform specific tasks.
- **Data Processing:** Serverless architecture is well-suited for data processing tasks, such as real-time analytics and batch processing.
- **API Backends:** Serverless functions can serve as lightweight backends for APIs, handling requests and returning responses quickly.

3.5 Case Study: Serverless Adoption

FaaS (Function as a Service) platforms, such as AWS Lambda, exemplify the adoption of serverless architecture. Companies like **Coca-Cola** have leveraged AWS Lambda to build event-driven applications that process user requests and automate workflows. By adopting a serverless model, Coca-Cola has significantly reduced operational costs and improved the agility of its development processes.

4. The Integration of AI and Machine Learning

4.1 The Impact of AI and ML on Software Architecture

Artificial Intelligence (AI) and Machine Learning (ML) are transforming how applications are designed and developed. These technologies enable software to learn from data, make predictions, and automate decision-making processes.

4.2 Key Considerations for AI and ML in Software Architecture

- **Data Management:** AI and ML applications rely on large volumes of data. Designing an architecture that supports data collection, storage, and processing is essential.
- **Model Deployment:** The architecture must accommodate the deployment of trained ML models, allowing them to be integrated into applications seamlessly.
- **Scalability:** AI and ML workloads can be resource-intensive. Ensuring that the architecture can scale to meet demand is critical for performance.

4.3 Benefits of Integrating AI and ML into Software Architecture

- **Enhanced User Experience:** AI-powered applications can provide personalized recommendations, improve search functionality, and automate customer support.
- **Improved Decision-Making:** Organizations can leverage data-driven insights to make informed decisions and optimize business processes.
- **Automation of Repetitive Tasks:** AI and ML can automate mundane tasks, allowing teams to focus on higher-value activities.

4.4 Use Cases for AI and ML in Software Architecture

- **Predictive Analytics:** Applications that analyze historical data to predict future trends or behaviors.
- **Natural Language Processing (NLP):** Applications that process and understand human language, such as chatbots and virtual assistants.
- **Computer Vision:** Applications that analyze and interpret visual data, enabling use cases like image recognition and facial detection.

4.5 Case Study: AI and ML Adoption

Companies like **Google** leverage AI and ML across their product suite, from search algorithms to automated image recognition. Google's cloud platform provides tools and services that allow organizations to build AI and ML capabilities into their applications, democratizing access to powerful data-driven insights.

5. Containerization and Orchestration

5.1 Understanding Containerization

Containerization is a lightweight form of virtualization that allows applications and their dependencies to be packaged together in isolated environments known as containers. This approach ensures consistency across different environments, from development to production.

5.2 Key Benefits of Containerization

- **Portability:** Containers can run consistently across various environments, making it easier to deploy applications.
- **Resource Efficiency:** Containers share the host operating system, resulting in lower overhead compared to traditional virtual machines.
- **Isolation:** Each container operates independently, allowing for better resource allocation and management.

5.3 The Role of Orchestration

Container orchestration tools (e.g., Kubernetes, Docker Swarm) automate the deployment, scaling, and management of containerized applications. Orchestration is essential for managing complex applications composed of multiple containers.

5.4 Benefits of Container Orchestration

- **Automated Scaling:** Orchestration tools can automatically scale applications based on demand, optimizing resource usage.
- **Load Balancing:** Orchestrators distribute traffic across multiple containers to ensure high availability and performance.
- **Service Discovery:** Orchestration tools enable containers to find and communicate with each other, simplifying inter-service communication.

5.5 Case Study: Containerization Adoption

Spotify has adopted containerization to streamline its development and deployment processes. By utilizing Docker containers and Kubernetes for orchestration, Spotify has improved its ability to deliver new features quickly while maintaining high levels of performance and reliability.

6. Edge Computing

6.1 What is Edge Computing?

Edge computing refers to processing data closer to the source of generation rather than relying on centralized data centers. This approach reduces latency and bandwidth usage, enabling real-time data processing and analysis.

6.2 Key Characteristics of Edge Computing

- **Proximity to Data Sources:** Edge computing processes data at or near the location where it is generated, reducing the distance data must travel.
- **Real-Time Processing:** By processing data at the edge, organizations can achieve faster response times and support time-sensitive applications.
- **Decentralization:** Edge computing promotes a decentralized architecture, distributing processing power across various locations.

6.3 Benefits of Edge Computing

- **Reduced Latency:** Edge computing minimizes latency by processing data closer to the source, enhancing the performance of applications that require real-time insights.
- **Bandwidth Optimization:** By processing data locally, edge computing reduces the amount of data transmitted to central servers, optimizing bandwidth usage.
- **Enhanced Reliability:** Edge computing can improve system reliability

by enabling applications to function independently of centralized data centers.

6.4 Use Cases for Edge Computing

- **IoT Applications:** Edge computing is ideal for IoT devices that generate large volumes of data, enabling real-time analytics and decision-making.
- **Autonomous Vehicles:** Edge computing processes data from sensors and cameras in real-time, allowing autonomous vehicles to make immediate decisions.
- **Smart Cities:** Edge computing supports smart city initiatives by processing data from various sensors and devices to enhance urban infrastructure.

6.5 Case Study: Edge Computing Adoption

GE Aviation has implemented edge computing in its aircraft engines to monitor performance in real-time. By processing data at the edge, GE Aviation can quickly analyze sensor data, detect anomalies, and make data-driven decisions to optimize engine performance and maintenance schedules.

7. Security in Software Architecture

7.1 The Growing Importance of Security

As cyber threats become more sophisticated, security must be a top priority in software architecture. Organizations need to build security into the software development lifecycle to protect sensitive data and maintain user trust.

7.2 Security by Design

Security by design involves integrating security practices into every stage of the software development process. This proactive approach helps identify and mitigate vulnerabilities early in the lifecycle.

7.3 Key Considerations for Security in Software Architecture

- **Threat Modeling:** Conducting threat modeling sessions to identify potential vulnerabilities and attack vectors.
- **Secure Coding Practices:** Implementing secure coding standards to prevent common vulnerabilities, such as SQL injection and cross-site scripting (XSS).
- **Automated Security Testing:** Incorporating automated security testing tools into the CI/CD pipeline to identify vulnerabilities before deployment.

7.4 Benefits of Emphasizing Security

- **Reduced Risk of Breaches:** Proactive security measures can significantly lower the likelihood of data breaches and cyberattacks.
- **Enhanced Compliance:** Organizations can better meet regulatory requirements and avoid legal penalties by prioritizing security.
- **Increased User Trust:** Demonstrating a commitment to security can enhance user confidence and loyalty.

8. The Role of Open Source in Software Architecture

8.1 The Open Source Movement

The open-source movement advocates for the free distribution and modification of software. Open-source software encourages collaboration and innovation, allowing developers to build upon existing solutions.

8.2 Benefits of Open Source in Software Architecture

- **Cost Savings:** Open-source solutions are often free to use, reducing licensing costs for organizations.
- **Community Support:** Open-source projects benefit from community-driven support, with developers collaborating to improve and maintain the software.
- **Flexibility and Customization:** Organizations can customize open-source solutions to meet their specific needs and requirements.

8.3 Popular Open Source Tools for Software Architecture

- **Kubernetes:** An open-source container orchestration platform that simplifies the deployment, scaling, and management of containerized applications.
- **Apache Kafka:** An open-source distributed streaming platform that enables organizations to build real-time data pipelines and streaming applications.
- **TensorFlow:** An open-source machine learning framework that provides tools for building and deploying AI and ML applications.

8.4 Challenges of Open Source in Software Architecture

While open-source solutions offer numerous benefits, organizations must also consider potential challenges, including:

- **Licensing Issues:** Understanding and complying with open-source licenses is essential to avoid legal issues.
- **Maintenance and Support:** Organizations may need to allocate resources to maintain and support open-source solutions.
- **Security Risks:** Open-source software can be vulnerable to security risks if not properly maintained and updated.

9. Preparing for the Future

9.1 Continuous Learning and Adaptation

As the software landscape evolves, organizations must foster a culture of continuous learning and adaptation. This involves:

- **Investing in Training:** Providing team members with opportunities to learn new technologies, methodologies, and best practices.
- **Encouraging Innovation:** Creating an environment that encourages experimentation and innovation, allowing teams to explore new ideas and solutions.

9.2 Embracing Emerging Technologies

Organizations should stay informed about emerging technologies that may impact software architecture, including:

- **Quantum Computing:** Exploring the potential of quantum computing to solve complex problems and enhance computational power.
- **5G Technology:** Adopting 5G technology to enable faster communication and enhanced capabilities for mobile and IoT applications.

9.3 Building Resilience

Building resilient software architectures is essential for navigating an increasingly complex and unpredictable environment. Strategies for resilience include:

- **Redundancy and Failover:** Implementing redundancy and failover mechanisms to ensure availability in the event of failures.
- **Monitoring and Observability:** Utilizing monitoring tools to gain insights into application performance and identify issues proactively.

- **Scalability and Flexibility:** Designing architectures that can scale horizontally and adapt to changing demands.

10. Conclusion

The future of software architecture is marked by rapid technological advancements, evolving methodologies, and a growing emphasis on quality, security, and collaboration. By embracing cloud-native architectures, microservices, serverless computing, AI and ML integration, and agile principles, organizations can build resilient, scalable, and high-quality software systems.

As the software landscape continues to evolve, the importance of documentation, testing, and collaboration will remain paramount. Organizations that prioritize continuous learning, innovation, and adaptability will be better positioned to thrive in an increasingly competitive environment.

In this rapidly changing world, software architects must remain vigilant and proactive, continuously seeking opportunities to improve and enhance their architectural practices. By doing so, they can create software systems that not only meet the needs of today's users but also anticipate the challenges and opportunities of tomorrow.

As we move forward, the principles and best practices outlined in this chapter will serve as a foundation for building the next generation of software architectures, paving the way for innovation and success in an ever-evolving digital landscape.

In the concluding chapter, we will summarize the key takeaways from this book and provide guidance for implementing the principles of software architecture in real-world projects, ensuring that readers are well-equipped to navigate the complexities of software development in the future.

Chapter 15: Implementing Software Architecture Best Practices in Real-World Projects

I mplementing software architecture best practices is essential for the successful development and maintenance of software systems. As software projects grow in complexity, architects and developers must ensure that their architectural decisions support not only the technical requirements but also the business goals. This chapter explores practical strategies for implementing software architecture best practices in real-world projects, covering key considerations, methodologies, and case studies that illustrate successful implementations. By adopting these practices, organizations can improve software quality, enhance maintainability, and foster collaboration among team members.

1. Understanding Software Architecture Best Practices

1.1 Defining Software Architecture Best Practices

Software architecture best practices refer to the principles and guidelines that promote effective design, development, and management of software systems. These practices encompass various aspects of software architecture, including design patterns, documentation, testing, security, and scalability.

By adhering to best practices, organizations can mitigate risks, improve code quality, and enhance the overall software development process.

1.2 Objectives of Software Architecture Best Practices

The primary objectives of implementing software architecture best practices include:

- **Ensuring Quality:** Best practices promote the development of high-quality software that meets user needs and expectations.
- **Facilitating Maintainability:** Well-structured and documented architecture simplifies maintenance and reduces the complexity of making changes.
- **Promoting Scalability:** By following best practices, organizations can design systems that scale effectively to accommodate growth and changing demands.
- **Enhancing Collaboration:** Best practices foster collaboration among team members by providing clear guidelines and standards for development.

1.3 The Impact of Best Practices on Software Development

Implementing software architecture best practices can significantly impact the success of software projects:

- **Reduced Technical Debt:** Adhering to best practices helps minimize technical debt, leading to more maintainable and extensible codebases.
- **Improved Time-to-Market:** A well-defined architecture enables teams to develop and deploy features more rapidly, reducing the time it takes to deliver value to users.
- **Increased Stakeholder Satisfaction:** High-quality software that meets requirements fosters trust and satisfaction among stakeholders, including users, business leaders, and clients.

2. Key Considerations for Implementing Best Practices

When implementing software architecture best practices, organizations should consider several key factors:

2.1 Alignment with Business Goals

Software architecture should align with the organization's strategic objectives. Architects must understand the business goals and ensure that architectural decisions support those objectives. This alignment helps prioritize features and design choices that deliver value to users and stakeholders.

2.2 Understanding Technical Requirements

Architects must have a deep understanding of the technical requirements of the software system, including performance, scalability, security, and maintainability. This knowledge allows architects to make informed decisions that balance technical constraints with business needs.

2.3 Stakeholder Involvement

Engaging stakeholders throughout the architecture design process is crucial for ensuring that the architecture meets user needs and expectations. Architects should involve stakeholders in discussions about requirements, trade-offs, and design choices to foster collaboration and buy-in.

2.4 Flexibility and Adaptability

Software architecture should be designed to accommodate change. As business requirements evolve, the architecture must be flexible enough to support new features and enhancements. Implementing modular design principles, such as microservices, can facilitate adaptability.

2.5 Documentation and Communication

Effective documentation is essential for conveying architectural decisions, design patterns, and best practices. Architects should prioritize documentation to ensure that team members have access to clear guidelines and reference materials. Additionally, fostering open communication among team members helps address questions and concerns related to the architecture.

3. Methodologies for Implementing Best Practices

3.1 Agile Methodologies

Agile methodologies, such as Scrum and Kanban, promote iterative development and flexibility. Implementing software architecture best practices within an Agile framework involves:

- **Continuous Feedback:** Regularly soliciting feedback from stakeholders helps refine architectural decisions and align with evolving requirements.
- **Incremental Design:** Adopting an incremental approach allows teams to implement architectural changes gradually, reducing risks associated with large-scale modifications.
- **Collaboration:** Agile emphasizes collaboration among team members, facilitating discussions about architectural choices and fostering shared understanding.

3.2 DevOps Practices

DevOps practices emphasize collaboration between development and operations teams, promoting a culture of continuous integration and delivery. Key practices for implementing best practices in a DevOps environment include:

- **Automated Testing:** Incorporating automated testing into the CI/CD pipeline ensures that architectural changes do not introduce defects.

- **Infrastructure as Code (IaC):** Using IaC tools (e.g., Terraform, Ansible) allows teams to manage infrastructure through code, promoting consistency and reproducibility.
- **Monitoring and Feedback Loops:** Implementing monitoring solutions provides insights into system performance, allowing teams to make data-driven decisions for architectural improvements.

3.3 Continuous Architecture

Continuous architecture is an approach that integrates architectural thinking into the development process. This methodology emphasizes:

- **Adaptive Design:** Architects continuously assess and adapt the architecture based on changing requirements and technology trends.
- **Incremental Refactoring:** Encouraging teams to refactor code and architecture incrementally ensures that improvements are made consistently over time.
- **Collaboration with Developers:** Involving developers in architectural discussions fosters a shared understanding of design decisions and promotes adherence to best practices.

4. Best Practices for Software Architecture Implementation

4.1 Design for Change

Designing for change involves creating a flexible architecture that can accommodate evolving requirements. Key strategies for achieving this include:

- **Modular Design:** Breaking the application into smaller, loosely coupled components (e.g., microservices) allows for independent development and deployment.
- **Use of Design Patterns:** Implementing design patterns, such as the Strat-

egy Pattern or Observer Pattern, promotes reusable and maintainable code.

- **Emphasizing Interfaces:** Defining clear interfaces between components enables teams to modify or replace components without affecting the entire system.

4.2 Prioritize Security

Security should be integrated into the software architecture from the outset. Best practices for enhancing security include:

- **Security by Design:** Implementing security measures during the design phase helps identify and mitigate vulnerabilities early in the development process.
- **Threat Modeling:** Conducting threat modeling sessions allows teams to identify potential security threats and develop strategies to address them.
- **Regular Security Audits:** Performing security audits and assessments helps ensure that the architecture remains secure as new features are added.

4.3 Comprehensive Documentation

Documentation plays a crucial role in ensuring that architectural decisions are understood and followed. Best practices for documentation include:

- **Clear and Concise Language:** Use clear, jargon-free language to make documentation accessible to all stakeholders.
- **Regular Updates:** Maintain documentation to reflect changes in the architecture and ensure it remains relevant and accurate.
- **Use Visual Aids:** Incorporate diagrams and visual representations to enhance understanding and retention of architectural concepts.

4.4 Emphasize Testing

Testing is essential for validating the architecture and ensuring software quality. Key testing practices include:

- **Automated Testing:** Implement automated tests at various levels (unit, integration, functional) to catch defects early in the development process.
- **Continuous Testing:** Integrate testing into the CI/CD pipeline to provide rapid feedback on the impact of code changes.
- **Load and Performance Testing:** Conduct load and performance testing to ensure that the architecture can handle expected user traffic and workload.

5. Case Studies of Successful Implementation

5.1 Case Study: Implementing Microservices at Amazon

Amazon has successfully adopted microservices architecture to enhance its e-commerce platform. By breaking the application into smaller, independent services, Amazon can scale its infrastructure based on demand. Each microservice is responsible for a specific business capability, allowing teams to develop and deploy features independently. This approach has enabled Amazon to achieve rapid innovation and deliver new features to customers quickly.

5.2 Case Study: Embracing Agile Practices at Spotify

Spotify has embraced Agile practices to streamline its development processes. By implementing cross-functional teams known as "squads," Spotify promotes collaboration among developers, designers, and product owners. The company emphasizes continuous feedback and iterative development, allowing teams to refine their architecture based on user feedback and changing requirements. This Agile approach has helped Spotify maintain its position as a leader in the music streaming industry.

5.3 Case Study: Adopting DevOps at Netflix

Netflix has successfully integrated DevOps practices into its software development lifecycle. By fostering a culture of collaboration between development and operations teams, Netflix can rapidly deploy new features and updates to its streaming platform. The company leverages automation and monitoring tools to ensure high availability and performance, allowing it to deliver an exceptional user experience. Netflix's commitment to continuous improvement and innovation has solidified its status as a leader in the entertainment industry.

6. Future Trends in Software Architecture

6.1 Increasing Adoption of AI and ML

As organizations continue to harness the power of AI and machine learning, software architecture will evolve to accommodate these technologies. Architects will need to design systems that can efficiently process large volumes of data and integrate machine learning models seamlessly.

6.2 Growth of Edge Computing

The rise of IoT and the need for real-time data processing are driving the adoption of edge computing. Software architects will need to consider how to distribute processing power and storage across edge devices while ensuring security and data integrity.

6.3 Evolution of Security Practices

As cyber threats become more sophisticated, security will remain a top priority for software architecture. Architects will need to adopt security practices that emphasize proactive measures and continuous monitoring to protect against potential vulnerabilities.

6.4 Embracing Low-Code and No-Code Development

The rise of low-code and no-code development platforms is changing the way software is built. Architects will need to adapt their practices to incorporate these tools while maintaining architectural integrity and quality.

6.5 Increased Focus on Sustainability

As organizations become more aware of their environmental impact, software architects will need to consider sustainability in their designs. This may involve optimizing resource usage, reducing energy consumption, and designing for long-term maintainability.

7. Conclusion

Implementing software architecture best practices is essential for the successful development and maintenance of software systems. By aligning architectural decisions with business goals, understanding technical requirements, and fostering collaboration among stakeholders, organizations can create resilient, scalable, and high-quality software.

As software development continues to evolve, architects and developers must remain adaptable and open to new methodologies, technologies, and trends. By embracing Agile practices, DevOps principles, and continuous improvement, organizations can position themselves for success in an increasingly competitive landscape.

The principles and strategies outlined in this chapter provide a roadmap for implementing software architecture best practices in real-world projects. By prioritizing collaboration, documentation, testing, and security, organizations can build software systems that not only meet user needs but also anticipate future challenges and opportunities.

As we conclude this exploration of software architecture, we will reflect on the key takeaways from the book and provide guidance for applying these principles in practice, ensuring that readers are equipped to navigate the complexities of software development in the future.

Conclusion: Navigating the Future of Software Architecture

As we conclude our exploration of software architecture, it is essential to reflect on the key themes, practices, and emerging trends discussed throughout the book. Software architecture is not merely a technical discipline; it is a crucial factor that influences the overall success of software projects. With the rapid advancements in technology, the increasing complexity of applications, and the evolving needs of businesses and users, architects and developers must be proactive in adapting to these changes.

1. Key Takeaways

1.1 The Importance of Software Architecture

Software architecture serves as the blueprint for building robust, scalable, and maintainable systems. It lays the foundation for meeting functional and non-functional requirements, such as performance, security, and usability. A well-defined architecture enhances collaboration among teams, facilitates communication with stakeholders, and ultimately leads to higher-quality software.

1.2 Best Practices for Software Architecture

Implementing best practices in software architecture is crucial for ensuring the success of software projects. Key practices include:

- **Aligning Architecture with Business Goals:** Architects must understand the strategic objectives of the organization and design systems that support those goals. This alignment ensures that architectural decisions are focused on delivering value to users and stakeholders.
- **Adopting Agile and DevOps Principles:** Embracing Agile methodologies and DevOps practices fosters a culture of collaboration, continuous improvement, and rapid delivery. These approaches allow teams to iterate quickly, respond to changing requirements, and deliver software that meets user needs.
- **Emphasizing Documentation:** Effective documentation is essential for conveying architectural decisions, design patterns, and best practices. Clear and comprehensive documentation supports knowledge transfer, aids onboarding, and enhances collaboration among team members.
- **Prioritizing Security:** Security should be integrated into the architecture from the beginning. Adopting a proactive security posture helps organizations identify and mitigate vulnerabilities, ensuring the protection of sensitive data and maintaining user trust.
- **Implementing Rigorous Testing:** Comprehensive testing strategies validate that the software meets its requirements and functions as intended. Continuous testing and automation facilitate rapid feedback on code changes, reducing the likelihood of defects.

2. Emerging Trends

2.1 Cloud-Native Development

Cloud-native architecture is becoming increasingly important as organizations seek to leverage the scalability and flexibility of cloud environments. Adopting microservices and containerization enables teams to develop and deploy applications more efficiently, fostering agility and innovation.

2.2 AI and Machine Learning Integration

The integration of AI and machine learning into software architecture is transforming how applications are designed and developed. Architects must consider how to effectively incorporate these technologies to provide enhanced user experiences and data-driven insights.

2.3 Edge Computing

As the demand for real-time processing grows, edge computing is emerging as a critical component of modern software architecture. By processing data closer to the source, organizations can reduce latency and improve performance, particularly for IoT applications.

2.4 Security Practices

As cyber threats become more sophisticated, security remains a top priority in software architecture. Organizations must adopt comprehensive security measures that encompass threat modeling, secure coding practices, and continuous monitoring.

3. Looking Ahead

As we look to the future of software architecture, it is clear that architects and developers must remain adaptable and open to change. The following strategies will help guide organizations as they navigate the complexities of software development:

- **Invest in Continuous Learning:** The technology landscape is constantly evolving. Organizations should prioritize ongoing training and professional development for team members to stay informed about emerging trends, tools, and methodologies.
- **Foster a Culture of Collaboration:** Encouraging collaboration between development, operations, and other stakeholders is essential for successful software architecture. Cross-functional teams promote knowledge sharing and align efforts toward common goals.
- **Focus on User-Centric Design:** Software architecture should prioritize the needs of users. Involving end-users in the design process and gathering feedback can help ensure that the final product meets their expectations.
- **Embrace Innovation:** Organizations should create an environment that encourages experimentation and innovation. Allowing teams to explore

new ideas and technologies can lead to breakthroughs that enhance software architecture.

4. Final Thoughts

In an era marked by rapid technological advancements and increasing demands for high-quality software, software architecture plays a pivotal role in determining the success of projects. By adhering to best practices, embracing emerging trends, and fostering a culture of collaboration and innovation, organizations can build resilient, scalable, and high-performing software systems.

As you move forward in your journey as a software architect or developer, remember that the principles and practices outlined in this book are not just theoretical concepts but practical strategies that can be applied to real-world projects. By prioritizing quality, security, and user satisfaction, you can contribute to creating software that not only meets the demands of today but also anticipates the challenges and opportunities of tomorrow.

In conclusion, the future of software architecture is bright, filled with opportunities for growth and innovation. By equipping yourself with the knowledge and skills to navigate this evolving landscape, you can play a crucial role in shaping the future of software development and delivering exceptional value to users and organizations alike.